A SEMANTIC AND STRUCTURAL ANALYSIS OF 2 THESSALONIANS

SIL International

Semantic and Structural Analysis Series

John Banker, General Editor

A SEMANTIC AND STRUCTURAL ANALYSIS OF 2 THESSALONIANS

Revised Edition

John Callow

SIL International

Revised Edition
© 1982, 2000 by SIL International

Library of Congress Catalog No. 00-108047
ISBN: 1-55671-111-5
Printed in the United States of America

All Rights Reserved
No part of this publication may be reproduced, stored in a retrieval system, or transmitted in any form or by any means—electronic, mechanical, photocopy, recording, or otherwise—without the express permission of SIL International, with the exception of brief excerpts in journal articles or reviews.

Copies of this and other publications of SIL International may be obtained from

International Academic Bookstore
7500 West Camp Wisdom Road
Dallas, TX 75236, USA

Voice: 972-708-7404
Fax: 972-708-7363
E-mail: academic_books@sil.org
Internet: http://www.sil.org

TABLE OF CONTENTS

Preface 7

0. General Introduction: The Theory and Presentation of Semantic and Structural Analyses 9
0.1 The Theory on which a Semantic and Structural Analysis is Based 9
0.1.1 Semantic Units in a Hierarchical System 9
0.1.2 The Features of a Semantic Unit 10
0.2 The Presentation of the Semantic and Structural Analysis (SSA) 11
0.2.1 The Communication Situation 11
0.2.2 The Overview 11
0.2.3 The Presentation and Discussion of the Units 12
0.2.3.1 The Order for the Presentation of the Units 12
0.2.3.2 The Unit Titles 12
0.2.3.3 The Unit Themes... 12
0.2.3.4 The Unit Displays 13
0.2.3.5 The Unit Discussions.. 16
0.3 The Use of the Semantic and Structural Analysis 17

The Chart of Communication Relations... 19

1. The Introduction to the Semantic And Structural Analysis of Second Thessalonians 21
1.1 The Communication Situation 21
1.1.1 The Participants... 21
1.1.2 The Occasion for Writing.. 21
1.2 The Overview 22
1.2.1 The Constituent Organization of 2 Thessalonians 22
1.2.2 The Thematic Outline of 2 Thessalonians 22

2. The Presentation and Discussion of the Semantic Units of Second Thessalonians 25

2 Thessalonians 1:1–3:18 (Epistle) 25
Epistle Constituent 1:1–2 (Paragraph).. 26
Epistle Constituent 1:3–3:16a (Division) 29
    Division Constituent 1:3–12 (Section) 31
        Section Constituent 1:3–4 (Paragraph) 33
        Section Constituent 1:5–10 (Paragraph) 37
        Section Constituent 1:11–12 (Paragraph)... 47
    Division Constituent 2:1–17 (Section) 52
        Section Constituent 2:1–12 (Paragraph Cluster).. 54
            Paragraph Cluster Constituent 2:1–3a (Paragraph).. 56
            Paragraph Cluster Constituent 2:3b–5 (Paragraph) 59
            Paragraph Cluster Constituent 2:6–8 (Paragraph) 62
            Paragraph Cluster Constituent 2:9–12 (Paragraph) 67
        Section Constituent 2:13–14 (Paragraph)... 71
        Section Constituent 2:15 (Propositional Cluster) 75
        Section Constituent 2:16–17 (Paragraph)... 77
    Division Constituent 3:1–5 (Section) 80
        Section Constituent 3:1–2 (Paragraph) 81
        Section Constituent 3:3–5 (Paragraph) 83
    Division Constituent 3:6–16a (Section).. 86
        Section Constituent 3:6–11 (Paragraph) 88
        Section Constituent 3:12 (Propositional Cluster)... 92

Section Constituent 3:13 (Propositional Cluster) 93
Section Constituent 3:14–15 (Paragraph) 95
Section Constituent 3:16a (Propositional Cluster) 97
Epistle Constituent 3:16b–18 (Paragraph) 99

Bibliography 101

PREFACE

This Semantic Structure Analysis of 2 Thessalonians is a development of initial analyses produced by a succession of students taking the Greek III course at the International Linguistics Center, Dallas— Ernest Chun (1975), Robert Sterner (1976), and Ronald P. Hood (1979). They, together with an independent (unpublished) analysis by Bruce Moore (undated), provided the present author with a detailed identification and justification of the semantic units of paragraph size and larger, and a good start with the propositional representation of the Greek grammar and lexicon. In addition, the author has benefited from the extensive exegetical comments prepared by Dr. John Werner (1976–77), and from the thorough discussion of the whole book—displays and notes—with Michael Kopesec prior to publication. Thanks are also due to Dr. David Clark for his careful review and comments.

There is much to recommend 2 Thessalonians as one of the first books to be considered by a translator who is beginning to work with the New Testament epistles: it is relatively short, it is relatively free from complex and difficult passages, and it has much in it to strengthen and encourage a church that is facing persecution. It is the desire of all who have been involved in the production of this volume that its use will greatly help the translator with the exegetical component of the translation task.

John Callow
Dallas, Texas
March 1982

The present edition is basically the same as the original one, but has been slightly revised and updated by John Banker with the technical help of Richard Blight and Elaine Beekman.

ABBREVIATIONS USED IN UNIT DISPLAYS

(emph)	emphatic
(exc)	exclusive
exem.	exemplary
(inc)	inclusive
neg.	negative
(pl)	plural
(sg)	singular

0. GENERAL INTRODUCTION: THE THEORY AND PRESENTATION OF SEMANTIC AND STRUCTURAL ANALYSES

0.1 The theory on which a semantic and structural analysis is based

This volume is an analytical commentary on Paul's second letter to the church in Thessalonica, which is based on a theory of semantic structure set forth in "The Semantic Structure of Written Communication" (Beekman, Callow, and Kopesec 1981). It has been prepared with the needs of the Bible translator particularly in view. Like other commentaries, it aims to arrive at the meaning that the original writer intended to communicate to the original recipients. It differs from most other commentaries, however, in that it is consciously based on a theory of the structure of meaning. Consequently, a consistent and comprehensive approach to the analysis of the meaning is applied to the total document, whether that meaning is conveyed by the smallest segments of the written communication (i.e., morphemes or words) or by the largest segments (i.e., the major constituents of the document or the whole document itself).

The title *A Semantic and Structural Analysis of Second Thessalonians*, has been carefully chosen. The term "structure" is meant to indicate that 2 Thessalonians is regarded as a document consisting of a coherent grouping of constituent parts. Each of these constituents, in turn, consists of coherent groupings of yet smaller constituents, and so on. These constituents, of whatever size or complexity, are identified and then (apart from the concepts, the smallest constituents of all) they are described as to their role or function within the total structure and as to their relationship to other constituents. As a structural analysis, the focus of this approach is also on the most important ("prominent") information being communicated by the document as a whole, and by its larger constituents; and on its overall organization.

The term "semantic" draws attention to the concern of this approach with meaning. It assumes that, in a system of communication, meaning has priority over the forms used to convey it. This correlates well with the aim of Bible translators and expositors to determine the meaning intended by the original writers and to convey it to an audience of a time, place, culture, and language other than those of the original addressees.

The salient features of the theory on which this approach is based are summarized below (0.1.1 and 0.1.2).

0.1.1 Semantic units in a hierarchical system

Two main points of this theory are particularly relevant to the analysis presented in this volume. The first of these is that a well-structured written communication, such as the various books of the New Testament constitute, consists of *semantic units* arranged in a *hierarchical system*. That is to say, there are smaller semantic units, which are combined into larger semantic units, which in turn are combined into yet larger units, and so on (see, for example, the constituent organization display in 1.2.1).

There are three basic types of semantic units: the concept, the proposition, and the propositional configuration. The *concept* corresponds roughly to the word or phrase in grammar. It is typically a coherent grouping of semantic components which refers to or names a thing, an event, an attribute, or a relation in the world spoken of in the document being considered. Each concept may also have an expressive component of meaning, more commonly referred to as its connotation. The concept characteristically functions as a constituent of a proposition and has a role within it; but such roles, while part of the total theory, are little used in this analysis—the focus of interest is on the proposition and the propositional configuration.

The *proposition* corresponds roughly to the clause. However, in Koine Greek other grammatical forms are often used to represent a proposition. For example, nouns and adjectives may represent event propositions (e.g., "salvation" and "saving"). Similarly, phrases may represent propositions (e.g., "into the knowledge of God" representing the proposition "in order that people may know God"). The proposition is typically a coherent grouping of concepts which communicates an event (e.g., "Jesus overturned the tables") or a state (e.g., "Zacchaeus was a small man"). Broadly speaking, the proposition carries out one of three communication, or illocutionary, functions—it asserts, questions, or commands the event or state that it refers to. The constituents of a proposition (typically concepts) are linked together by a system of relations in which the constituents fulfill what have come to be called "case roles." (For a presentation of case roles, see Beekman, Callow, and Kopesec 1981, chapter 6).

The *propositional configuration* is a coherent grouping of propositions and/or other propositional configurations which are related to each other by a system of "communication relations." The extent of development of a particular discourse, combined with the human tendency to "package" or group things for more effective conceptual or cognitive control, has given rise to a number of typical groupings of propositional configurations. For narrative material, a typical hierarchy of propositional configurations is as follows: propositional cluster, paragraph, episode, scene, act, and part (ranging from small to large). In nonnarrative literature (such as the epistles), the more typical configurations encountered are propositional cluster, paragraph, section, division, and part.

Each type of configuration is defined in terms of its composition; that is, a division is a propositional configuration consisting of two or more constituents, at least one of which is a section; a section is a propositional configuration consisting of two or more constituents, at least one of which is a paragraph; etc. The subclassification of the propositional configurations is sensitive to other considerations as well. The general size and complexity of the unit is the main consideration. However, there are times when the size and complexity of the unit does not unequivocally decide the issue. In such cases, another factor comes into play—the distribution of the unit in the overall organization of the discourse. For example, two units of more or less the same complexity and size may be classed differently, because the one is functioning at a level in the overall structure that is characteristic of propositions, whereas the other is functioning at a level that is characteristic of paragraphs or larger units. The first could be regarded as a propositional cluster and the second as a paragraph.

0.1.2 The features of a semantic unit

The second main point of the theory that is especially relevant to a semantic and structural analysis such as this of 2 Thessalonians is that each semantic unit, no matter how small or how large, is characterized by six meaning features, grouped into three "analytical features" and three "holistic features."

Analytical features	Constituency	(Internal) Coherence	Prominence
Holistic features	Classification	(External) Coherence	Thematic content

The three *analytical* features enable the analyst to identify the semantic units in a written document, distinguishing one unit from another, to relate the units to each other, and to pick out the most important information that is communicated by each unit. The discussions of each semantic unit describe these particular features in detail. The three *holistic* features come into play in the overall characterization of a unit (as shown in the main label) and in the discussion of the purpose of the units.

Since the analytical features are more overtly involved in the process of analysis, they are discussed here in a little more detail. The feature of *constituency* refers to the fact that each semantic unit consists of other semantic units. Coherence has to do with how those constituent units combine with each other. They have to be referentially coherent, i.e., there is repetition of reference in the unit, whether by identical repetition, the use of synonyms or "pro" forms, or structural devices such as parallelism, chiasmus, and "sandwich structure." They have to be situationally coherent, i.e., the time-frame should be acceptable in the world being talked about, there should be expressive consistency, there should be overall illocutionary consistency. And the constituent units should be structurally coherent, i.e., the relations between any pair of units should be compatible with the content of those two units (again, in the world being talked about by the writer).

The third analytical feature, *prominence*, has to do with the relative degree of importance of information in a semantic unit. (Note that the determination of relative importance is not from a theological perspective, nor from an overall biblical perspective, but from the perspective of the development of the particular unit being analyzed.) Perhaps the most significant thing to be pointed out about the feature of prominence is the distinction between natural and marked (or special) prominence. *Natural prominence* is closely tied to the relational structure. In many binary pairs of relations, one of the two relations is naturally more prominent. For example, an exhortation is more prominent than the grounds it is paired with, the result is more prominent than the reason, and so on. *Marked prominence* is shown by special linguistic devices in the language being studied. For example, in Koine Greek, at the propositional cluster level, marked prominence is generally shown by a nontypical ordering of the clauses, or by a propositional cluster of lesser natural prominence being given the form that would be expected of a prominent cluster. At the propositional level, a frequent prominence-marking device is the placement of material in front of the verb. Marked prominence is used in the discourse for a variety of reasons, some of which are: topic identification and maintenance, contrast, intensification, and highlighting.

0.2 The presentation of the semantic and structural analysis (SSA)

In this section of the general introduction, a description of the various parts of the SSA will be given. The reader may wish to refer to the table of contents for an outline of these parts.

0.2.1 The communication situation

Every written discourse is produced by someone in a particular place, time, and set of circumstances; and it is directed toward someone in a particular place, time, and set of circumstances. There is also, generally, a specific aspect of this "situational context" that motivates the writer to address the reader. The nature of the physical, cultural, and psychological setting, the relationship between the writer and the intended reader(s), and the particular details of the motivating factors have a very obvious influence on the shape that the written communication takes. Those factors in the communication situation which are regarded as particularly significant for the adequate understanding of the document being analyzed are presented in this part of the SSA.

0.2.2 The overview

The main function of the overview is to provide the user with a bird's-eye-view of the whole discourse, so that, as he works with smaller portions of the discourse, he will be able to refer to the overview, either mentally or directly, and thereby keep track of the place that the portion he is working with has in the whole discourse. The overview itself generally involves very little in the way of discussion, since all of the units, from the entire discourse down to the paragraph, and in some cases propositional clusters, are handled in considerable detail as each individual unit is presented and dealt with.

An overview consists of a constituent organization display and a thematic outline. The constituent organization display provides the reader with a visual presentation of the way that the constituents of the discourse are hierarchically arranged with respect to one another. No attempt is made in this display to state the contents or the semantic roles of the constituents.

The thematic outline provides a summary of the prominent information in the discourse. The theme statements of each of the units are arranged in an outline format, conforming to their hierarchical arrangement. The role that each unit plays in the configuration of which it is a part is identified explicitly in the unit title.

0.2.3 The presentation and discussion of the units

0.2.3.1 The order for the presentation of the units

The units are described in the order that the following diagram indicates:

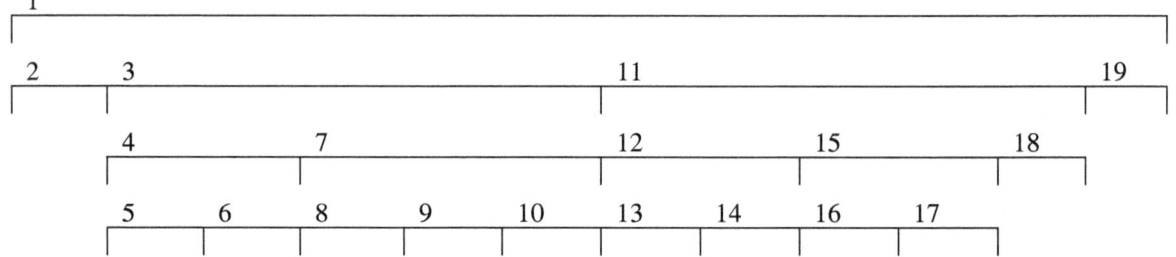

Such an order accomplishes two things. First, it allows each unit to be discussed in terms of the higher-level framework into which it fits; and second, it allows the units to be discussed in the order in which they occur. In other words, the order for the discussion is sensitive both to the hierarchical and the linear aspects of the contents.

0.2.3.2 The unit titles.

The units are titled in such a way as to provide the user with a good deal of information. Take, for example, a title in an SSA such as "DIVISION CONSTITUENT 3:1-9 (Paragraph: Specific$_3$ of 1:6-7)." In this example "DIVISION CONSTITUENT" indicates that the unit is an immediate constituent of a configuration which, by its composition, is a division. In the parentheses, "Paragraph" tells the user that the unit being discussed is, by its composition, a paragraph. This is followed by an indication of the role that that paragraph is playing in the relational structure of the division in which it is functioning. In this particular example paragraph 3:1-9 is said to serve as the third specific of 1:6-7, another constituent of the division which includes 3:1-9.

An important fact is illustrated in this particular title. Note that the unit is compositionally a paragraph, and yet it is said to be a principal constituent of a division. A paragraph is more commonly a principal constituent of a section, and a section is more commonly a principal constituent of a division. A strict hierarchical approach would require that every principal constituent of a division be labeled a section, but the approach used in the SSA establishes how a unit is classified (paragraph, section, etc.) primarily on the basis of its composition, not exclusively on the basis of the organizational level on which the unit is functioning. A higher-level unit, viewed compositionally, consists of a configuration of two or more principal constituents, one of which *must* be a unit of the next lower compositional level, while the other constituent(s) may be of any level lower than the configuration itself. For example, a division must consist of at least two principal constituents, one of which must be a section, while the others may be sections, paragraphs, propositional clusters, or propositions. More commonly, the principal constituents of a division are sections and paragraphs, but occasionally a propositional cluster functions as a principal constituent of a division (see, for example, 2:15), and very rarely a proposition does.

0.2.3.3 The unit themes

Following the title of each unit is its theme statement. The theme is an expression of the information content that is regarded as the most prominent in the unit. This generally consists of the proposition, propositional cluster, or constituent theme statement that corresponds with the left-most capitalized label in the relational structure diagram, along with any other constituent or portion of a constituent (e.g., a thematic motif) which is marked by special devices as prominent. (It should be noted that theme statements are not given in the strict propositional form used in the displays themselves, but certain concessions are made to normal English usage, such as the use of the infinitive after verbs such as "want," "cause," etc.)

0.2.3.4 The unit displays

The displays of the units are divided into two parts, the left side showing how the constituents of the unit are related to one another and the right side expressing the meaning or contents of those constituents.

In the *left-hand side*, entitled "RELATIONAL STRUCTURE," a multi-layered display of the relations between the constituents that make up the unit is given. The relational labels derive from those in *Translating the Word of God* (Beekman and Callow 1974, chapter 18) as subsequently modified and elaborated in "The Semantic Structure of Written Communication" (Beekman, Callow, and Kopesec 1981, chapter 8). (In this revised edition some of the labeling has been updated.) The system of relations has been included here (see chart on page 19) for the convenience of the reader. Since 2 Thessalonians is hortatory and expository in discourse type (genre), the stimulus-response group of labels, which apply more particularly to conversation and narrative discourses, are not included in the chart.

The fact that many of the relational structure displays are multi-layered illustrates that, in the structure of a communication unit, the constituents that comprise it group together in a variety of configurations and patterns; that is, groupings of constituents as well as single constituents may function as the highest-level (or principal) constituents of the unit. Then each of the groupings may be broken down, or further analyzed, into single constituents or groupings. And then those groupings may be further analyzed into single constituents or groupings, and so on. The left-most set of relational labels in a relational structure display shows the way the unit divides into its principal constituents. The next layer shows how some or all of those principal constituents are further analyzed into smaller ones. The next layer after that shows how some or all of those constituents may be further analyzed into smaller ones, and so on. The degree of delicacy, i.e., the number of levels or layers used to display the unit, is largely a matter of the analyst's judgment as to what is useful for communicating the organizational development of the unit under question. Obviously, the more that can be displayed with a single chart, without rendering the chart unwieldy or overly atomistic, the better. At the finer levels of delicacy, the decision as to whether to separate the constituents and display the relationships between them is based on a number of factors:

1. The extent or complexity of development of one constituent may require several layers of relations to display its organization, whereas another constituent may require only one or two layers because it is so briefly stated. For example, in the relational structure display for 2 Thess. 1:3–4 note that one of the two principal constituents has only one additional layer of relations, whereas the other has three.

2. Closely related to the previous point is the relative significance of the different relations. Often another layer is added in order to display an argumentation relationship, but not to display a supplementation, clarification, or orientation relationship. Also, addition relations at the lower levels of delicacy are usually not sufficient cause for adding further layers in the display. (This practice is not obviously illustrated in this SSA.)

3. The organizational level, on which a particular element is functioning often enters into the decision. For example, quite frequently an orienter-content relationship is not elaborated in the relational structure display. The orienter "they will believe" in 2 Thess. 2:11b has not been separated from its content (what they believed) in the display of 2:9–12. However, the orienter in 1:11b has been displayed separately. This is due primarily to the fact that prayer orienters are highly significant in the introduction to the body of a Pauline epistle, but also because the content consists of four constituents, so that combining the orienter with the following content would make an unduly large undifferentiated unit, which is avoided whenever possible.

Taking the case of an orienter again, it may be necessary to show it as a separate constituent in the display so as to avoid giving a false representation of the structure, particularly the grouping. For example, if the content introduced by an orienter is grouped with two conjoined CONTENTS, one of which is developed at some length whereas the other is not, the developed CONTENT will be displayed to several layers, which entails its being presented as a separate grouping in the display. This means that the orienter and the undeveloped CONTENT will also have to be displayed as separate (small) groupings.

Or the orienter itself may be developed, and hence require presentation separately in the display (e.g., 2 Thess. 2:16–17).

There are a number of notational conventions used in the relational structure display that need to be described:

1. The relational labels of one layer are aligned horizontally with the nuclear element of the next lower layer, as illustrated by the following example:

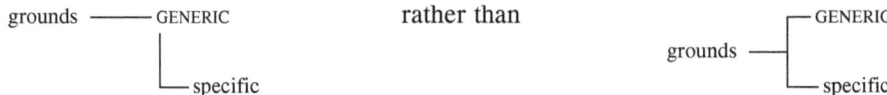

Although this violates the symmetry that a standard tree diagram would display, it is a particularly useful visual convention. By aligning the labels in this manner, the user can quickly determine all of the relationships that any given constituent has. By following the horizontal line which extends leftward from a specific constituent identified in the right-hand side of the unit display, the relational labels pertinent to it will be encountered. To determine its main support role, one simply has to follow that line to the lowercase label, and that will be its support role. For example, using the display of 2 Thess. 3:6–11, notice that by following the horizontal line leftward from constituent 3:8b, three relational labels are encountered. The first one is NUCLEUS. It indicates that 3:8b is supported by 3:8a, a contrast, and by 3:8c–9c, two purposes and a negated reason. The second label that is encountered along that horizontal line moving leftward from 3:8b is in uppercase letters—SPECIFIC. This label indicates that the grouping 3:8a–9c, of which 3:8b is the NUCLEUS, is supported by 3:7a and 7b, the first being a topic orienter and the second being a generic statement of which 3:8b, the nuclear proposition, is a more specific statement. Then continuing to the left along the horizontal line a grounds$_1$ label is encountered. This indicates that the grouping 3:7–9, and more particularly its NUCLEUS (3:8b), functions as a (first) grounds for the main nucleus, the EXHORTATION (3:6).

2. Uppercase and lowercase labels are used to graphically enhance the contrast between nuclear and support elements in a given set of related constituents. The prominent element in the set is written in uppercase letters, and the support relation labels are written in lowercase letters. Occasionally, the support element in a set of related units is marked for prominence by special devices. In such cases both the nuclear label and the support label will be written in uppercase letters. Consider, for example, the display of 2:1–17, which has the principal relational structure SPECIFIC (neg.)-grounds-NUCLEUS-means. Normally, the specific label would be in lowercase letters, but since this support item is marked as prominent in the surface structure, it is analyzed as having equal prominence with the NUCLEUS of the unit.

3. A grouping of related constituents at any given layer of delicacy consists of a minimum of two units, at least one of which will be labeled in uppercase letters. Quite commonly, two or more support constituents relate to a common nuclear constituent. An example of this can be seen in the display of 3:6–11, where the NUCLEUS constituent (3:8b) is supported by a (preceding) contrast (negative) (3:8a), and by a (following) purpose (3:8c), negated reason (3:9a), and purpose (3:9b–c). This means that 3:8b, the NUCLEUS, is simultaneously functioning as the contrast (positive) of 3:8a, and the means of 3:8c and 3:9b–c, and the result of 3:9a.

4. Subscript numbers are used to indicate units related by addition. The addition relationship of conjoining is illustrated in the relational structure display of 1:5–10. Note that 1:6a–b and 7a–b are labeled grounds$_1$ and grounds$_2$, indicating that they are conjoined grounds in support of the NUCLEUS (1:5). The other addition relationship, alternation, is exemplified in the display of 2:1–3a, where there are three alternative conditions (2:2c, 2d, and 2e) supporting the CONSEQUENCE (2:2a–b).

The *right-hand side* of the displays, entitled "CONTENTS" represents the semantic content as unambiguously and as completely as possible.

If the unit under discussion is compositionally larger than a paragraph (i.e., section, division, etc.), then the "contents" consists of the theme statements for the constituents that make up the unit. See, for example, the display of 1:3–3:16a. However, if the unit under discussion is a paragraph or a propositional cluster, then the "contents" consists of a "propositionalized" representation of the semantic information contained in the Greek text of the unit.

A word needs to be said at this point concerning the nature and representation of propositions and concerning the general principles for the "propositionalization" of the contents of a unit. Technically, the proposition is a *semantic* entity; it underlies, or is signaled by, the surface structure forms. It is a grouping of "concepts," one of which expresses the state or event notion to which the others are related by a set of relations commonly called "case." Also, the proposition has one of the three basic illocutionary or communicative functions: assertion, question, or command. Since the proposition is not a surface structure (i.e., grammatical and phonological) entity, it cannot properly be equated with any specific surface structure form. However, for practical purposes it has been necessary to work out a means of representing the propositions and their interrelationships as completely and unambiguously as possible and in a way that causes the least distortion in conveying the underlying semantic content. This is what is referred to as the "propositionalized" content.

Some of the principles involved in this type of representation are the following:

1. One of the most important principles asserts that the grammatical form of the representation should match as closely as possible the class of the semantic units (Beekman and Callow 1974:282). This means that semantic events are represented consistently by verbs and not by nouns (e.g., "salvation," grammatically a noun, is represented by some form of the verb "to save"). Semantic things (animate beings and inanimate objects) are consistently represented by nouns. Semantic attributes of things (e.g., "largeness," "the color green," etc.) are consistently represented by adjectives (e.g., "big," "green," etc.) modifying nouns; attributes of events (e.g., "quickness") are represented by adverbs (e.g., "quickly") modifying verbs; and attributes of attributes (e.g., "heightened intensity of hotness of a thing") are consistently represented by adverbs (e.g., "very (hot)"). Semantic relations, such as those between concepts (the case relations) and those between propositions, paragraphs, etc. (the communication relations), are represented by surface structure devices which signal how one unit is related to another. These often are simple conjunctions (e.g., "because" indicating a reason relationship, "in order that" indicating a purpose relationship, etc.). Most often the relationship signaled by the particular relator will be self-evident. However, when there is ambiguity, the relational structure on the left side of the display disambiguates the conjunction by indicating explicitly how the relation has been analyzed. Frequently, it is necessary to represent the relation with a relator word along with the repetition of some previously given information which more clearly indicates the precise unit to which it relates.

2. Passive forms are avoided in the propositionalized content, except when they are used to retain the topic focus of the unit. However, whenever a passive form is used, the doer of the action is stated in italics; thus, "you were saved" may be propositionalized as "you were saved *by God*."

3. Italics are used to indicate implicit material that has been made explicit, as, for instance, "*by God*" in the previous example. Languages differ considerably as to what information must be signaled explicitly and what can be left implicit; so in the propositional representation of the contents, the implicit information is given, but it is given in italics so that the user will be aware that it is not explicit in the surface structure. One of the main functions of italics is to supply the significant participants of event propositions. For example, the abstract noun "salvation" could be represented propositionally as "*God* saves *people*." Only "saves" occurs without italics since the only referent that is explicitly represented in the surface structure text is the event concept of the proposition. Italics also enclose information repeated for linking purposes and information added to disambiguate pronominal references, to supply omissions due to ellipsis, and to clarify obscurities due to presuppositions and common cultural knowledge (e.g., in the display of 1:1–2, constituent 1:1 includes "town" after "Thessalonica" to make explicit what would have been clearly understood by the original readers concerning the place named Thessalonica).

4. In addition, figures of speech, such as dead metaphor, metonymy, synecdoche, litotes, hyperbole, etc., are expressed nonfiguratively. Rhetorical questions are expressed in a straightforward manner, as assertions or commands, depending on their communication function. For live metaphors, an attempt is generally made to retain the item used figuratively, while adding information that sets forth the content intended to be communicated by the figure. Wherever it is considered that there is a connotative component associated with a figure of speech, which is not captured in the propositional rewrite, the figure is identified after the rewrite by three capital letters in square brackets, e.g., [HYP], [RHQ].

5. The representation of the contents in a propositionalized form also involves the verbalization of relative prominence in the contents. The conjunctions and other relation-marking devices serve not only to indicate the relations between propositions and propositional configurations, but also to indicate relative prominence. But such things as topic focus and the highlighting of information or motifs, also need to be represented. The general approach is to use standard English prominence-marking devices to represent this aspect of the meaning of the text. However, there are some features of prominence which are recognized in the Greek text but which cannot be easily represented in written English. These are simply discussed in the "notes" portion of the unit discussions.

Each of the constituents in the right-hand side of the display is identified as follows. At the beginning of each constituent the chapter(s) and verse(s) that it represents are indicated. If any given verse is divided between two or more constituents, then lowercase letters are used to indicate such subdivisions of verses (e.g., 1:12a; 1:12b; 1:12c; etc.). There are cases where, for purposes of clarity of presentation, the order of the constituents in the display differs from their order of occurrence in the Greek surface structure. Such a situation does not affect the identifying labels for subdivided verses; they always conform to the display order.

Finally, it should be noted that conjoined units are not grouped in the display, so as to avoid extra layering in the diagram. Consider, for example, the two purposes (1:12a and 1:12b–c). These are conjoined and are grouped together (as shown in the Greek grammar by the use of a single ὅπως 'in order that' introducing them and a καί 'and' linking them). So, strictly speaking, they could be diagrammed as follows:

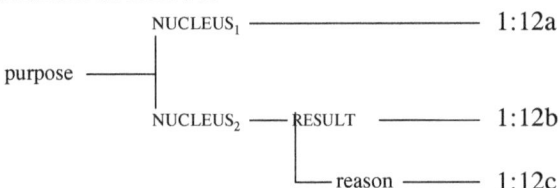

Diagramming it this way, however, introduces an extra layer into the display, as can readily be seen; so the convention of using subscripted numbers has been adopted to keep the layering within reasonable bounds. The subscripts 1, 2, etc. indicate the relation of conjoining of constituents with the same relation to some other one.

0.2.3.5 The unit discussions

Following the display of the unit there is a discussion of the factors that entered into the decisions represented in the SSA. The discussion centers around (a) evidence for the identification of the unit, (b) evidence for the theme (and purpose) of the unit, and (c) notes regarding decisions made concerning the relational structure and/or the propositionalization of the contents. (In the original edition of the SSA of 2 Thessalonians, these discussions followed the above order, but in this revised edition the notes on the individual verses (c) come first so that they will be closer to the display for easier reference for the user.)

The discussions dealing with *evidence for the identification of the unit* set forth features which are used to establish the unit as a distinct and discrete whole and which set the unit apart from contiguous ones. Such discussions are subtitled "Boundaries and Coherence" in this SSA.

The discussions dealing with *evidence for the theme of the unit* (entitled "Prominence and Theme") set forth factors which are involved in the derivation of the theme statement. Evidence from the relational structure of the unit and other natural and special prominence marking features enter into this discussion. Of special importance in this discussion is the justification of elements in the theme statement which derive from constituents other than the main nucleus of the unit.

In some cases, the *purpose* of a unit will be discussed. This is more likely in the case of higher-level units, but possibly it will be done also for some paragraphs. Since in epistle material purpose is closely related to the theme of a unit, such discussions will be combined with discussions of the theme of the unit.

The *notes* part of the unit discussions includes two types of notes:

1. Notes on the relational structure of the unit. Often there are points in the relational structure of the unit that need explanation, justification, and/or the presentation of alternative possibilities. Such matters are dealt with in the notes.

2. Decisions on information content. The final decisions on the meaning of the text and the manner of expressing that meaning in propositional form are often not as clear and unequivocal as one would like them to be. At many such points, commentators differ quite radically concerning the intended meaning. In the display, an attempt has been made to decide between the options on objective linguistic grounds. The bases for many such decisions are presented in the notes. At times no conclusive evidence has been found for clearing up one of these exegetical ambiguities. In such cases, the option that appears to the analyst to be the most likely one is included in the display of the unit, and the alternative interpretations are discussed in the notes.

The bibliography attached to the SSA indicates the source materials consulted by the analyst(s). These keep the analyst aware of the different exegetical choices at a given point, and often indicate factors to be weighed in reaching an exegetical decision. However, in many cases, the factor is reworked and reworded by the analyst(s) to conform to the general linguistic orientation of an SSA. Hence, detailed acknowledgement of individual sources for every factor involved in each exegetical decision is generally not practicable, but tends to be done where a minority or unusual factor or decision is being discussed. Also, it is borne in mind that the primary audience is translators, whose focus is of necessity more on the exegetical decisions and the reasons for them, than on where the ideas may have come from, since it is the exegetical decision that is going to be reflected in the translation.

0.3 The use of the semantic and structural analysis

The person engaged in Bible translation is very likely to ask himself how a technical commentary of this nature should be used, and how it relates to other aids available to him. The SSA represents a step beyond the standard exegetical or critical commentary. A cursory comparison of commentaries will reveal a wide variety of alternative interpretations at numerous points in the text. A serious attempt is made in the SSA to arrive at a specific interpretation, taking into account all the factors which are considered to be relevant—the words used, the grammatical constructions involved, the relational structure, the theme of the units, the overall purpose of the document, etc. The SSA, therefore, represents the fruit of careful reasoning by a number of scholars. Consequently, it is recommended to be used by the translator as a special type of commentary, in which the needs of the translator have been uppermost in the minds of those preparing it. It should, however, be used along with other commentaries and versions, and where there is obvious agreement, the translator can move ahead with confidence. Where the display appears to depart from the versions or commentaries, or where a number of alternatives occur, then the discussion that accompanies the displays should be carefully studied to see what factors led to the decision represented in the display. The user should then be in a good position to form his own factually-based judgment as to the best interpretation.

Although the needs of those translating God's Word are the primary motivation in the production of this sort of commentary, it is certainly the hope of all those involved in their production that others would find it useful, too. Pastors and teachers, who desire to expound the Scriptures faithfully and to base their messages on a careful exposition of the text, should find the SSA a real help as they wrestle with the meaning of God's Word. Here the arguments for and against differing interpretations are given. Also, there are various types of information in the SSA which are not consistently found in other commentaries; for example, which of the various statements are related to each other, how they are related to each other, and which are the most important. The careful overall analysis of the book is of considerable help, too.

And what is of help to a pastor or teacher is also of help to the serious Bible student who wishes to study the Word for his own profit. It will help anyone leading a Bible study in which there is a genuine desire to study the meaning of the text; and it should certainly help any Bible college or seminary student. Hopefully, Bible college and seminary professors will find the approach and its underlying theory stimulating to interact with, as presenting suggestions for new approaches to the careful exegesis of the Biblical materials.

It has been the practice of all who are involved in the many hours of work required to produce an SSA to use every means at their disposal—the standard reference works, the commentaries, the insights of linguistics, the theory of semantic structure, etc.—so as to arrive at as accurate an understanding of God's Word as is possible in our present state of knowledge. For all who share this same concern, this commentary should prove useful.

Chart of Relations

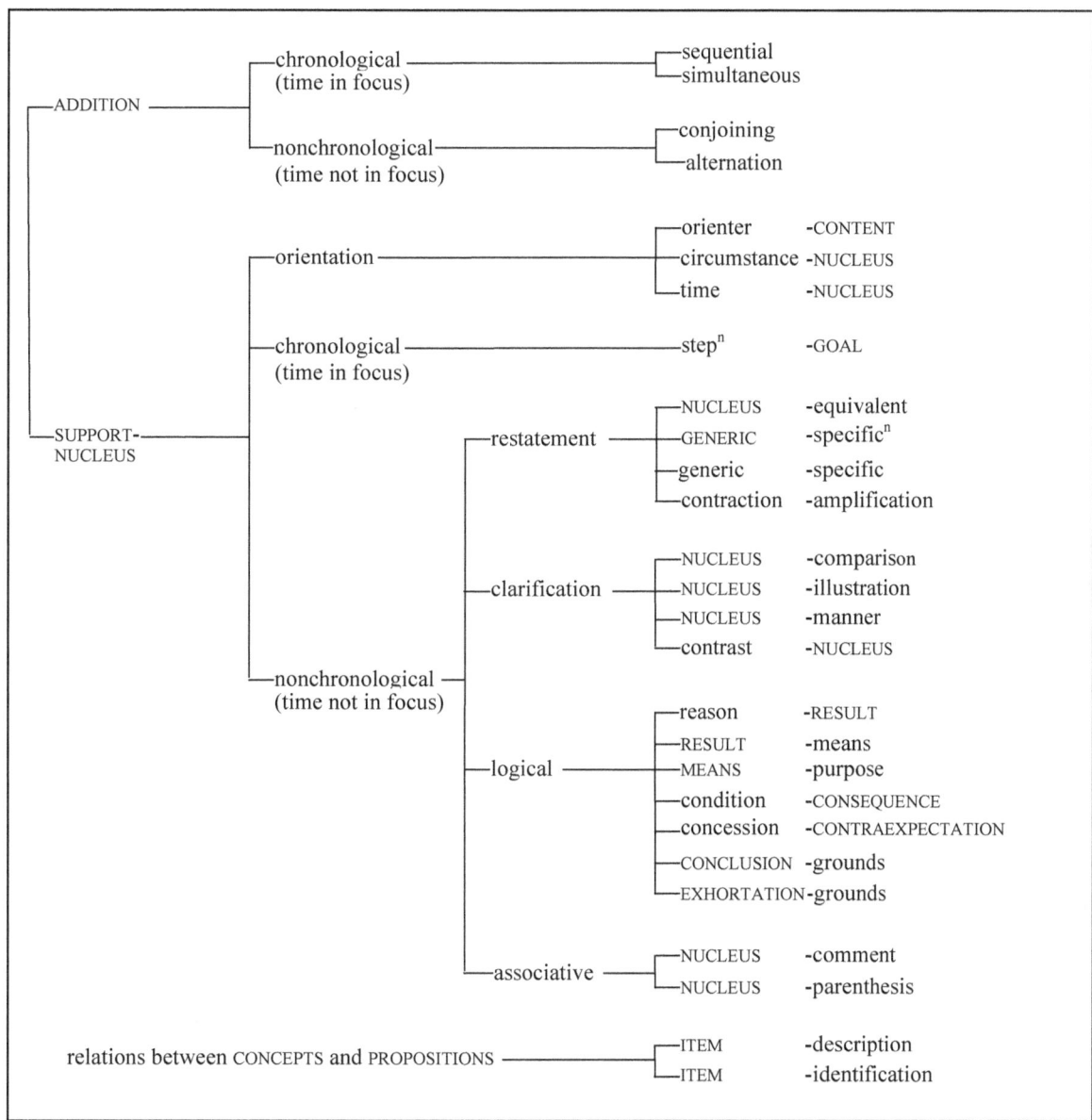

Notes on the Chart of Relations:
1. The relations are to be read horizontally, e.g., orienter-CONTENT, circumstance-NUCLEUS.
2. Since Second Thessalonians is nonnarrative, the narrative, or chronological, relations are not all included in this chart.
3. The relations are given in the order in which they are most commonly found in the Greek of the New Testament; thus an orienter usually precedes the CONTENT which it orients.
4. The naturally prominent member of a paired relation is shown in caps. There does not seem to be a natural nucleus for contraction-amplification; the prominence will be determined by the context.
5. It should be noted that devices marking prominence can be used by the author to make the less prominent member of a pair as prominent as the one which is naturally prominent.
6. In a conjoined relation where one (or more) of the constituents is less prominent, that constituent will be labeled either "conjoined" or "nucleus" (in lower case).

1. THE INTRODUCTION TO THE SEMANTIC AND STRUCTURAL ANALYSIS OF SECOND THESSALONIANS

1.1 The communication situation

It is an integral part of the theory of the semantic structure of written communication that a written document reflects the situation in which it was written—the general historical situation and the particular situation of the writer(s) and recipient(s). It will reflect the personality, beliefs, circumstances, etc., of the writer and the knowledge and assumptions that the writer brings to the document concerning the circumstances, etc., of the readers. Further, the overall purpose of the document will be closely related to the particular situation which gave rise to it. These features of the communication situation are least obvious in a third person narrative; most obvious in such materials as an autobiography or a personal letter. Since 2 Thessalonians is in this latter category, it is of value to the translator to be familiar with the communication situation, since it provides the background against which various exegetical decisions are made.

1.1.1 The participants

Second Thessalonians was sent by Paul, Silvanus, and Timothy, as the first five words of the Greek tell us. Silvanus (Σιλουανός) is regarded as a variant form of Silas (Σίλας), which is the form used by Luke throughout Acts. (Σιλουανός is used by Paul here and in 2 Cor. 1:19 and 1 Thess. 1:1; Peter also uses this form in I Pet. 5:12.) Silas first appears in Acts 15:22 and 27 where he is one of two leading (Jewish) Christians mentioned in the letter from the Jerusalem church to the Gentile believers, and who are sent with it, as a result of which he joined Paul and Barnabas at Antioch, and exercised his prophetic ministry there (Acts 15:32). When Paul fell out with Barnabas, it was Silas he chose to accompany him on his second missionary journey (15:40), which eventually reached Thessalonica (17:1–9), after the dramatic events in the jail at Philippi. At Thessalonica, after the trouble caused by the Jews, he had to leave by night with Paul .

Timothy (Τιμόθεος) is first introduced in Acts in connection with this second journey, as Paul chose Timothy to accompany him when he reached Derbe and Lystra. From then onwards (until Luke joined them), there were three in the missionary team. However, Timothy is not mentioned again by Luke until the missionary team is in Berea, the next place evangelized after Thessalonica. It seems very likely that his was a junior, trainee role, so he was not directly involved in the persecutions in Philippi, Thessalonica, and Berea. But since he is included among the senders of this letter, it seems only reasonable to assume that he had played his more minor part in the founding of the church at Thessalonica.

Throughout the letter, the writers are referred to as "we," except in 2:5 (which probably implies that Paul was the principal teacher), and, significantly, in 3:17, where Paul sends his personal greetings in his own handwriting, as an authentication of the genuineness of the letter. It would seem, therefore, that Paul personally dictated the letter, in his role as the leader of the missionary team, so that he is writing on behalf of the three of them, Silas and Timothy being one with him in what he said.

The church itself was predominantly a Gentile one—mainly Greeks presumably, but there were a good many Romans living in the town also. Some Jews were converted, but the majority were not, and were very hostile to Paul and Silas, not only causing them to leave Thessalonica, but pursuing them to Berea also. Thus, this particular church was born in the midst of persecution, but it was a lively and vigorous church, spreading the gospel throughout much of (what is now) Greece.

1.1.2 The occasion for writing

When Paul and Silas (and probably Timothy, too) left Thessalonica, they went to Berea, which Paul had to leave hurriedly, only this time he left Silas and Timothy behind (Acts 17:14). They evidently, as he had requested (17:15), rejoined him in Athens, but it would seem he had sent them off again quite quickly, Silas probably to Berea, and Timothy to troubled Thessalonica (1 Thess. 3:1–3). They rejoined him at Corinth (Acts 18:5), and 1 Thessalonians is Paul's very relieved and joyful letter when he heard that the Thessalonian Christians were standing firm in the midst of continuing persecution.

However, probably not too long afterwards, very likely from news brought back by those who had taken 1 Thessalonians to Thessalonica, Paul heard that the Thessalonian church was still being persecuted (2 Thess. 1:4-6); he heard, too (3:11), that the tendency of some of the believers there to abandon working for their living, already noted in 1 Thess. 4:11 and 5:14, had continued in spite of what he had written; and there was evidently a rumor going round, claiming to have Paul's backing, that the Day of the Lord had already come, which was causing confusion, excitement, and unsettledness. So Paul, on behalf of the missionary team, wrote a second, shorter letter dealing with these various matters. In other words, as he wrote, Paul had in mind the practical problems of continuing persecution and some refractory, idle members; and the doctrinal question of refuting the rumor that the Lord had already returned.

Meanwhile, between the first and second letters, Paul himself had run into opposition in Corinth. In 1 Thess. 5:25, he simply says, "Brethren, pray for us." But in 2 Thess. 3:2, he is asking them to pray that God would rescue him and the others from evil men. This probably refers to the opposition of the Jews at Corinth to him and his message, mentioned in Acts 18:6 and 18:12-17.

1.2 The overview

1.2.1 The constituent organization of 2 Thessalonians

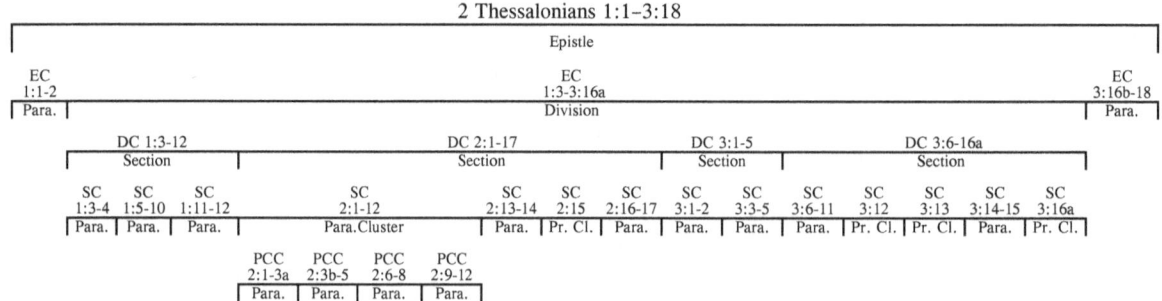

Abbreviations: EC: Epistle Constituent; DC: Division Constituent; SC: Section Constitutent;
PCC: Paragraph Cluster Constuent; Para.: Paragraph; Pr. Cl.: Propoositiional Cluster

1.2.2 The thematic outline of 2 Thessalonians

2 THESS. 1:1-3:18 (Epistle) Continue believing the body of teaching which was committed to you by us(exc). In particular, do not be quickly troubled in mind and alarmed by any message that the Day of the Lord has already come. And disassociate yourselves from every brother who refuses to work.

EPISTLE CONSTITUENT 1:1-2 (Paragraph: opening of the Epistle) We(exc), Paul, Silas, and Timothy, are sending this letter to you, who are the company of God's people in Thessalonica. We(exc) pray that God will continue to bless you.

EPISTLE CONSTITUENT 1:3-3:16a (Division: Body of the Epistle) Continue believing the body of teaching which was committed to you by us(exc). In particular, do not be quickly troubled in mind and alarmed by any message that the Day of the Lord has already come. And disassociate yourselves from every brother who refuses to work.

DIVISION CONSTITUENT 1:3-12 (Section: introduction to the Body) We(exc) thank God very frequently that you are believing in the Lord Jesus more and more. And we(exc) are praying very frequently for you that God will consider you worthy to receive that to which he summoned you.

SECTION CONSTITUENT 1:3-4 (Paragraph: Nucleus₁ of 1:3-12) We(exc) thank God very frequently that you are believing in the Lord Jesus more and more.

SECTION CONSTITUENT 1:5-10 (Paragraph: conjoined to 1:3-4 and 1:11-12) God will judge all people justly. Specifically, he will publicly declare that you are worthy to enter that place where he will rule his people forever.

SECTION CONSTITUENT 1:11-12 (Paragraph: Nucleus$_2$ of 1:3-12) We(exc) are praying very frequently for you that God will consider you worthy to receive that to which he summoned you.

DIVISION CONSTITUENT 2:1-17 (Section: Nucleus$_1$ of the Body) Continue believing the body of teaching which was committed to you by us(exc). in particular, do not be quickly troubled in mind and alarmed by any message that the Day of the Lord has already come.

SECTION CONSTITUENT 2:1-12 (Paragraph Cluster: specific (neg.) of 2:15) Do not be quickly troubled in mind and alarmed by any message that the Day of the Lord has already come.

PARAGRAPH CLUSTER CONSTITUENT 2:1-3a (Paragraph: Nucleus of 2:1-12) Do not be quickly troubled in mind and alarmed by any message that the Day of the Lord has already come.

PARAGRAPH CLUSTER CONSTITUENT 2:3b-5 (Paragraph: Nucleus of 2:3b-12; grounds for 2:1-3a) The Day of the Lord will come only after that time when the man who will sin very greatly will have been revealed by God.

PARAGRAPH CLUSTER CONSTITUENT 2:6-8 (Paragraph: circumstance$_1$ of 2:3b-5) This man will be revealed by God when he who is now preventing him from being revealed will have been removed by God.

PARAGRAPH CLUSTER CONSTITUENT 2:9-12 (Paragraph: circumstance$_2$ of 2:3b-5) When this man will be present, he will completely deceive those who will perish.

SECTION CONSTITUENT 2:13-14 (Paragraph: grounds for 2:15) God chose you and summoned you in order that you might be saved and glorified.

SECTION CONSTITUENT 2:15 (Propositional Cluster: Nucleus of 2:1-17) Continue believing the body of teaching which was committed to you by us(exc).

SECTION CONSTITUENT 2:16-17 (Paragraph: means of 2:15) We(exc) pray that our(inc) Lord Jesus Christ himself will encourage you and cause you to continue doing and speaking what is good.

DIVISION CONSTITUENT 3:1-5 (Section: conjoined to 2:1-17 and 3:6-16a) Pray that more and more people will believe the message about our(inc) Lord Jesus. Our(inc) Lord Jesus will cause you to continue to be steadfast and he will protect you from the evil one.

SECTION CONSTITUENT 3:1-2 (Paragraph: Nucleus$_1$ of 3:1-5) Pray that more and more people will believe the message about our(inc) Lord Jesus.

SECTION CONSTITUENT 3:3-5 (Paragraph: Nucleus$_2$ of 3:1-5) Our(inc) Lord Jesus will cause you to continue to be steadfast and he will protect you from the evil one.

DIVISION CONSTITUENT 3:6-16a (Section: Nucleus$_2$ of the Body) We(exc) command you to disassociate yourselves from every brother who refuses to work.

SECTION CONSTITUENT 3:6-11 (Paragraph: Nucleus of 3:6-16a) We(exc) command you to disassociate yourselves from every brother who refuses to work.

SECTION CONSTITUENT 3:12 (Propositional Cluster: conjoined to 3:6-11) We(exc) command those brothers who are not working to support themselves by settling down and working.

SECTION CONSTITUENT 3:13 (Proposition Cluster: conjoined to 3:6-11) You others, do not stop doing what is right because you are discouraged.

SECTION CONSTITUENT 3:14-15 (Paragraph: conjoined to 3:6-11) Publicly identify any brother who does not obey what we(exc) have written in this letter and do not associate with him.

SECTION CONSTITUENT 3:16a (Propositional Cluster: conjoined to 3:6-11) We(exc) pray that our(inc) Lord Jesus himself will give peace to you always and in every situation.

EPISTLE CONSTITUENT 3:16b–18 (Paragraph: closing of the Epistle) In closing, we(exc) pray that our(inc) Lord Jesus will continue to bless you all. I, Paul, am greeting you and I am writing this myself in order that you may know that I, Paul, have sent this letter.

2. THE PRESENTATION AND DISCUSSION OF THE SEMANTIC UNITS OF 2 THESSALONIANS

2 THESSALONIANS 1:1–3:18 (Epistle)

THEME: Continue believing the body of teaching which was committed to you by us(exc). In particular, do not be quickly troubled in mind and alarmed by any message that the Day of the Lord has already come. And disassociate yourselves from every brother who refuses to work.

RELATIONAL STRUCTURE	CONTENTS
opening	1:1–2 We(exc), Paul, Silas, and Timothy, are sending this letter to you, who are the company of God's people in Thessalonica. We(exc) pray that God will continue to bless you.
BODY	1:3–3:16a Continue believing the body of teaching which was committed to you by us(exc). In particular, do not be quickly troubled in mind and alarmed by any message that the Day of the Lord has already come. And disassociate yourselves from every brother who refuses to work.
closing	3:16b–18 In closing, we(exc) pray that our(inc) Lord Jesus will continue to bless you all. I, Paul, am greeting you and I am writing this myself in order that you may know that I, Paul, have sent this letter.

COHERENCE OF THE EPISTLE

This epistle shows the three characteristic parts of a Pauline epistle, namely, the opening, the body, and the closing. The body itself consists of four constituents (see the organizational chart, 1.2.1), which are described in detail in connection with the discussion of the body.

The coherence of the body, or, the evidence for its unity, is also discussed in connection with the body itself. Suffice it to say here that the unity is partly structural, i.e., it consists of the material other than the opening and closing, and it is partly referential, in that there are frequent references to we(exc) throughout, and to you(pl). This epistle, also, is distinguished by its frequent references to the Lord Jesus (for its length, proportionately more than any other Pauline epistle).

EPISTLE CONSTITUENT 1:1–2 (Paragraph: opening of the Epistle)

THEME: *We(exc), Paul, Silas, and Timothy, are sending this letter to you, who are the company of God's people in Thessalonica. We(exc) pray that God will continue to bless you.*		
RELATIONAL STRUCTURE		CONTENTS
NUCLEUS₁		1:1 *We(exc),* Paul, Silas, and Timothy, *are sending this letter* to *you*, who are the company *of God's people* in Thessalonica *town*, and who belong to God, *who is* our(inc) Father, and *who belong to* Jesus Christ, *who is* our(inc) Lord.
NUCLEUS₂		1:2 *We(exc) pray that* God, *who is* our(inc) Father, and Jesus Christ *who is* our(inc) Lord, *will continue to* act graciously toward you and *will continue to* cause you to have *peace.

Verses 1:1–2 of this epistle follow the established pattern for the beginning of a letter that was used in Paul's time: the writer identifies himself and those to whom he is writing, and then greets them, which greeting in Paul's letters takes the form of a prayer that God would bless the recipients. Formally, the writer gives his name in the nominative case; the recipients are in the dative case; and the prayer is verbless in form and without any expressed performative. The body of the letter then follows with the use of the first finite verb in the first person (singular or plural).

The formal opening of 2 Thessalonians is analyzed as a paragraph consisting of two propositional clusters in the relation of conjoining.

NOTES

Because such letter beginnings were formalized, there was a lot of implicit information, and this inevitably poses problems for the exegete, and especially the translator. Note the following points:

1:1 *We(inc),* **Paul, Silas, and Timothy,** *are sending this letter* **to** *you*, **who are the company** *of God's people* **in Thessalonica** *town*, **and who belong to God,** *who is* **our(inc) Father, and** *who belong to* **Jesus Christ,** *who is* **our(inc) Lord.** There is no verb relating the writer(s) and the recipients. The most natural is the verb "to write," and this also agrees with the cases used in the Greek—nominative for the writer(s), and dative for the recipients. An alternative verb is that used in the display, "to send," which would also fit in with the cases used. There are two matters arising in connection with the verb "to write" which translators should bear in mind:

1. In this context, "to write" does not mean "to pen," "to physically write," but rather to provide the contents of the letter. It is clear from the next to last verse of this letter that Paul only took the pen at that point and personally wrote his own greeting; the rest of the letter was, presumably, dictated by Paul.

2. Who actually composed the letter? The Greek makes no formal distinction between Paul, Silas, and Timothy, except for the order in which they are presented. Further, "we" forms are used throughout this letter, except for 2:5 and 3:17. In this respect, this letter differs from 1 Corinthians, where Sosthenes is associated with Paul in the formal opening, but the very first verb is in the singular. Hence, it is generally (and reasonably) assumed that, although Paul was the author of this letter, he drew no sharp distinction between himself, on the one hand, and Silas and Timothy on the other. They were the evangelistic team who had brought the gospel to Thessalonica, and the letter is written as from the team, rather than just from Paul personally. The fact that he does not refer to his apostleship in the opening confirms this. If, however, the translation requires reference to a single writer, for either grammatical or semantic reasons, then Paul would be that writer, as he is the one who gives his personal greeting at the end as proof of the genuineness of the letter. A possible propositional form would be: I, Paul, together with Silas and Timothy, am writing this letter to you...

The form "Silas" is used, which is the form used by Luke in Acts. Paul (and Peter) use the longer form Σιλουανός. It is suggested for translation that "Silas" be used here, and the longer form footnoted, or referred to in a glossary.

Paul refers to the Thessalonian believers with the term ἐκκλησία 'church', as he does also in 1 and 2 Corinthians, Galatians (in the plural), and 1 Thessalonians. Best points out that the Septuagint uses ἐκκλησία to refer to God's people in the Old Testament, whether actually in assembly or not, so for the Greek-speaking Jew, and for any Gentile God-fearers, ἐκκλησία already had religious overtones. But for the average pagan Gentile, it simply referred to an assembly of the people in a particular locality (Luke so uses the term in Acts 19:32, 39, 41). It is essentially a collective term for referring to believers, or God's people. The display has sought to reflect this with "the company of God's people."

The display uses "in Thessalonica *town*." Rather unusually, Paul has "of the Thessalonians," since he usually refers to the location itself. No semantic distinction appears to be intended, so the more usual Pauline form is given in the display.

The most difficult point exegetically in 1:1 is the expression "the church of the Thessalonians in God our Father and (the) Lord Jesus Christ." What does "in" mean here? It is probably the case, as suggested by several commentators and grammarians, that the "in" expression is added to distinguish the Christian church from a Gentile assembly and from Jewish congregations or synagogues. In general, Paul uses "in" with Christ to express spiritual union with the head of redeemed humanity, the second Adam; and with Lord to express believing in or belonging to, roughly corresponding to the modern sense of "Christian." Since nothing further is said to explain the expression, the following alternatives are all considered possible:

1. "Who are united to..." This is the generally preferred view. I cannot find, however, any other examples of Paul's using ἐν θεῷ 'in God' meaning this. (There are six instances of ἐν (τῷ) θεῷ apart from this passage. 1 Thess. 1:1 is the same, so only poses the same problem; Rom. 2:17 and 5:11 are the normal collocations after καυχάομαι 'to boast'; Eph. 3:9 is taken to mean "hidden by God," and 1 Thess. 2:2 "emboldened by God." The only possible passage where union with God could be referred to is Col. 3:3, your life is hidden with Christ in God," but the union is expressed by σύν 'with', as on a number of occasions in Colossians, and the context points to the sense "in the presence of God.")

2. "Who believe in..." While this makes good sense, Paul generally speaks of faith in the Lord Jesus, not in God, and while ἐν 'in' is used with the noun πίστις 'faith', the prepositions ἐπί and εἰς are the more normal collocations with the verb πιστεύω 'to believe'.

3. "Who belong to..." Normally, in these epistle openings, the ἐν 'in' phrase identifies the location in which the recipients of the letter lived. Since Paul has used the form Θεσσαλονικέων 'Thessalonians' here, no reference to a location is needed, and so the ἐκκλησία 'church' is identified by saying it is ἐν θεῷ πατρὶ ἡμῶν καὶ κυρίῳ Ἰησοῦ Χριστῷ 'in God our Father and (our) Lord Jesus Christ'. This is probably best represented by saying it "belongs to"; it is that ἐκκλησία 'church/assembly' which is God's and Christ's. It is this last view which is used in the display.

1:2 *We(exc), pray that* **God,** *who is* **our(inc) Father, and Jesus Christ** *who is our(inc)* **Lord,** *will continue to* **act graciously toward you and** *will continue to* **cause you to have *peace.** This verse is regarded as a prayer, but is expressed in a brief and stylized form. The question arises here, as it does also in the final verse of Paul's epistles, as to how "grace" (χάρις) should be understood. Does it have its full theological sense of God giving his blessings freely to those who can in no way merit them? Or does it have the more general sense of "bless," "do good to," "act kindly towards"? There is not as much difference as would appear at first sight, as, for Paul, "grace" is the word that characterizes all God's favorable attitudes and actions towards sinful men. Since it is a formal greeting, an expression should be chosen by translators which is appropriate to a greeting. (It is possible that Paul adapted the general Greek word for "greetings," χάρειν, to make it a specifically Christian greeting—this would be appropriate for a translation, also.)

To some extent, the same issue arises with the word "peace" (εἰρήνη). Again, it is very widely held that the choice of this word reflects the Hebrew greeting of *shalom* 'peace', which expresses much more than lack of strife, or even inner peacefulness. Rather it conveys the idea of "spiritual prosperity," "enjoying God's blessing," general "blessedness." In other words, it is the reciprocal of God's blessing, the recipients' state of blessedness. Hence, in translation some general word should be used that is appropriate for *spiritual* blessedness rather than material prosperity, which is not a New Testament emphasis.

BOUNDARIES AND COHERENCE

The initial boundary of this unit coincides with the opening of the discourse, and its final boundary is marked by the formalized "greeting" which characteristically ends the opening of letters.

Its unity lies primarily in its function as the opening of the letter; there are also, however, the twofold references to God the Father and our Lord Jesus Christ.

PROMINENCE AND THEME

The opening does not have a theme in the sense of a proposition that is further developed by argument, illustration, etc.; in this context, it is simply identical with the most prominent information—the identity of the senders, the identity of the recipients, the activity of sending the letter, and the prayer for blessing. In the theme statement, the verb "to bless" is used in its most generic sense to cover the two more specific prayers in the greeting, and "God" is used as a generic term to represent the specific persons of the Godhead referred to in the prayer.

EPISTLE CONSTITUENT 1:3–3:16a (Division: Body of the Epistle)

THEME: Continue believing the body of teaching which was committed to you by us(exc). In particular, do not be quickly troubled in mind and alarmed by any message that the Day of the Lord has already come. And disassociate yourselves from every brother who refuses to work.

RELATIONAL STRUCTURE	CONTENTS
introduction	1:3–12 We(exc) thank God very frequently that you are believing in the Lord Jesus more and more. And we(exc) are praying very frequently for you that God will consider you worthy to receive that to which he has summoned you.
NUCLEUS₁	2:1–17 Continue believing what you were taught by us(exc). In particular, do not be quickly troubled in mind and alarmed by any message that the Day of the Lord has already come.
conjoined	3:1–5 Pray that more and more people will believe the message about our(inc) Lord Jesus. Our(inc) Lord Jesus will cause you to continue to be steadfast and he will protect you from the evil one.
NUCLEUS₂	3:6–16a We(exc) command you to disassociate yourselves from every brother who refuses to work.

BOUNDARIES AND COHERENCE

The opening boundary of the body is clearly marked by the change, without formal marker (i.e., by asyndeton), from the formalized opening, with its lack of any verb forms, to the first verb form, εὐχαριστεῖν 'to thank'. In addition, there is the occurrence of the first vocative, ἀδελφοί 'brothers', and the first performative, εὐχαριστεῖν ὀφείλομεν 'we ought to thank'. Each of the major constituents of the body of this epistle begins with this vocative and a performative (for fuller details, see below), and the beginning of the body is indicated by the first occurrence of these opening signals.

The end of the body, however, is not as clear as it is in most of the other epistles. This problem is discussed in detail in connection with the boundaries and coherence of the final constituent (3:6–16a) and also of 3:16a. Suffice it to say here that with 3:16b the typical unconnected and verbless ending of a letter begins, while 3:16a is the prayer which closes 3:6–16a, very similar in form to the prayers which close earlier constituents. Hence, the body is considered to close with 3:16a.

The most obvious coherence phenomenon in the body is the constant "we-you" orientation throughout, as would be expected in a letter. But apart from this and references to "God" and "the Lord Jesus Christ" (especially the latter) throughout the letter, there is little lexical or relational coherence for the body as a whole, even where it might be expected. For example, the first two constituents have several references to the return of the Lord Jesus, but even so, apart from "that day" in.1:10, and "the day of the Lord" in 2:2, there is no common vocabulary. The unity of the body is essentially a functional unity of being the body, as distinct from the formal opening and closing.

STRUCTURE, PROMINENCE, AND THEME

It will be easier to follow the discussion of the prominence and theme if the overall structure of the body is presented first.

Second Thessalonians is a very clearly structured epistle. The body of the epistle consists of four sections, each characterized by three initial phenomena, and by one closure phenomenon. The initial features are:

1. The vocative ἀδελφοί 'brothers' (1:3; 2:1; 3:1, 6);
2. A first person plural performative ("we ought to thank God" (1:3); "we request you" (2:1); "we command you" (3:6); for 3:1, see the discussion below); and
3. Apart from the first section, which has no conjunction (as in all of Paul's letters), each section is introduced either by δέ (2:1; 3:6) or τὸ λοιπόν 'as for the other matters' (3:1).

The closure feature is a prayer (1:11–12; 2:16–17; 3:5; 3:16a), the form of the prayer in the last three cases being obviously similar. (It should be stressed that it is the combination of all *four* of these features that marks the boundaries of a section; paragraphs may show combinations of up to three of them.)

The opening section (1:3-12) is the introductory part of the body, in which Paul, Silas, and Timothy thank God for the Thessalonian believers, encourage them in persecution, and pray for them. The remaining three sections are essentially hortatory, containing commands addressed to the Thessalonian believers (note the performatives listed under feature 2 above), and, in the absence of any connectives other than δέ and τὸ λοιπόν, are considered to be conjoined.

The questions of prominence and theme, then, are concerned with the three sections which follow the introduction. It is in this context that section 3:1-5 stands out as somewhat different. It does not start with a formal performative, like the other two, but with the direct command, "pray for us"; it is not introduced by δέ, but by τὸ λοιπόν, variously considered to mean "finally, next, as for the other matters"; and it is very brief and undeveloped compared to the other sections. How to interpret τὸ λοιπόν in this letter is far from clear, but the above evidence would indicate that 3:1-5 is of less prominence than the two sections on either side of it.

The other two sections are considered to be equally prominent. The theme of 2:1-17 consists of a generic-specific pair, the generic command being marked by the only use of οὖν in this epistle (2:15), and by having its own vocative; the specific has a typical performative orienter-content theme statement. This is also true for the theme of 3:6-16a. Hence, the theme of the body is considered to consist of the conjoined themes of 2:1-17 and 3:6-16a, dealing with the two major matters of the epistle. In the statement of the body theme, all orienters have been dropped and replaced by direct commands.

DIVISION CONSTITUENT 1:3-12 (Section: Introduction to the Body)

THEME: We(exc) thank God very frequently that you are believing in the Lord Jesus more and more. And we(exc) are praying very frequently for you that God will consider you worthy to receive that to which he has summoned you.

RELATIONAL STRUCTURE	CONTENTS
NUCLEUS₁	1:3-4 We(exc) thank God very frequently that you are believing in the Lord Jesus more and more.
— conjoined	1:5-10 God will judge all people justly. Specifically, he will publicly declare that you are worthy to enter that place where he will rule his people forever.
NUCLEUS₂	1:11-12 We(exc) are praying very frequently for you that God will consider you worthy to receive that to which he summoned you.

BOUNDARIES AND COHERENCE

The beginning of this unit is clearly marked by:

a. the first finite verb, effectively a first person plural performative (εὐχαριστεῖν ὀφείλομεν 'we ought to thank' is considered to be broadly equivalent to the more usual εὐχαριστοῦμεν 'we thank');
b. the vocative ἀδελφοί 'brothers'; and
c. the switch to thanksgiving from the formal opening.

The end of this unit is shown as follows:

a. the formal parallelism between the opening "we ought to thank God always for you" (1:3) and "we pray always for you" in 1:11, which, in effect, forms a "performative" sandwich structure;
b. the lexical sandwich of reference to the Thessalonians' faith in 1:3 (ἡ πίστις ὑμῶν 'your faith') and in 1:11 (ἔργον πίστεως '(your) work of faith'); and
c. the switch of genre to hortatory material in 2:1.

The unity of 1:3-12 is also shown by some of the above evidence, in particular, the performative sandwich, and the fact that there is only one vocative for 1:3-12, the next occurring in 2:1. In addition, it is a very heavily "you" oriented passage: overt reference to "you" (by pronoun, verb ending, and vocative) occurs no less than seventeen times, almost twice a verse on the average. Along with the heavy emphasis on "you," there is an equally heavy emphasis on God and the Lord Jesus Christ; the former is overtly referred to eight times, the latter ten times. This is in marked contrast with the following unit (2:1-12).

In addition to the performative sandwich, there is a lexical sandwich of items drawn from the semantic domain of Christian character and activity. Verses 1:3 and 4 refer to the Thessalonians' faith, love, and steadfastness; and 1:11 refers to their goodness, good deeds, and faith.

PROMINENCE AND THEME

It will be clear from what has been said so far about this unit that it consists of three constituents—1:3-4, 5-10, and 11-12—and that the first and the last form a sandwich structure, being similar in a number of ways. This structure highlights a problem over which there is a considerable difference of analytical opinion: is the central unit (1:5-10) more or less prominent than the two outer units (1:3-4 and 1:11-12)? The answer has generally been "more prominent," so that the theme for this section has been sought for in 1:5-10.

In my opinion, this approach, though plausible, is wrong. The following are the reasons why I think this:

1. Such an analysis, in effect, ignores the fact that 1:3-12 constitutes the introductory part of the body in this particular letter. It is in 2:1, with the first occurrence of δέ, that Paul, as it were, gets down to actual business (cf. 1 Cor. 1:10). The introduction, in Paul's letters, is a heavily "we-you" oriented section, generally consisting of thanks to God for the Christian graces of the recipients, and sometimes also praying for them. This should be clearly reflected in the theme statement for this introductory section, but 1:5-10 is notably lacking in this "we-you" orientation. (In support of this, it could also be pointed

out that the only two independent finite verbs in 1:3–12 are the two performatives in 1:3 and 11.)

2. It is argued that the first and last constituents of this section are relationally supporting the middle one. This analysis is based on the mistake of treating tail-head linkages as if they were theme-to-theme linkages. Thus, in 1:4, reference is made to the steadfastness of the Thessalonian believers during their present persecutions. This fact, picked up by ἔνδειγμα 'evidence, proof' at the beginning of 1:5, and repeated again at the end of 1:5, is a grounds for the theme of 1:5–10. It is argued that this makes paragraph 1:3–4 the grounds of 1:5–10. But, in fact, reference to the sufferings of the Thessalonians is *not* thematic in 1:3–4, but only supports the theme, forming a transition from the one paragraph to the next. Similarly, the final paragraph, the prayer for the Thessalonians, is regarded as a means supporting 1:5–10. There is more plausibility in this suggestion and it seems the best analysis for the section-end prayers that occur later in this same epistle. But there are two good reasons against this analysis here in this first section:

   a. The prayer is introduced (after an opening phrase—see point b below) by καί 'and'. Since καί is used to join grammatical units of the same grammatical rank (word to word, phrase to phrase, clause to clause, etc.), the best analysis is that καί links this (prayer) performative with the thanks performative in 1:3.

   b. The prayer is also introduced by the phrase εἰς ὅ 'toward which'. The ὅ undoubtedly refers back to some or all of the preceding paragraph, and εἰς can certainly signal the relation of purpose. Hence, εἰς ὅ is taken to refer to 1:5–10 as the purpose, of which 1:11–12, the prayer, is the means. But, firstly, means is normally more prominent than purpose, so paragraph 1:5–10 would have to be marked in some way for prominence; and secondly, two other purposes are spelled out for the prayer in 1:11 and 12, one with a ἵνα 'in order that', and the other with a ὅπως, having much the same meaning here as ἵνα. It is most unlikely that the least strongly marked purpose, i.e., εἰς ὅ, would be more prominent than the clauses introduced by ἵνα and ὅπως. The εἰς ὅ, in fact, is better understood as giving a reason why Paul and Silas prayed that particular prayer so frequently for the Thessalonians.

The conclusion reached, then, is that paragraphs 1:3–4 and 1:11–12 are more prominent than the paragraph 1:5–10. The relation between them all is considered to be conjoining. The theme, then, of this introduction to the body of the epistle, is a simple conjoining of the themes of 1:3–4 and 1:11–12.

SECTION CONSTITUENT 1:3–4 (Paragraph: Nucleus₁ of 1:3–12)

THEME: We(exc) thank God very frequently that you are believing in the Lord Jesus more and more.

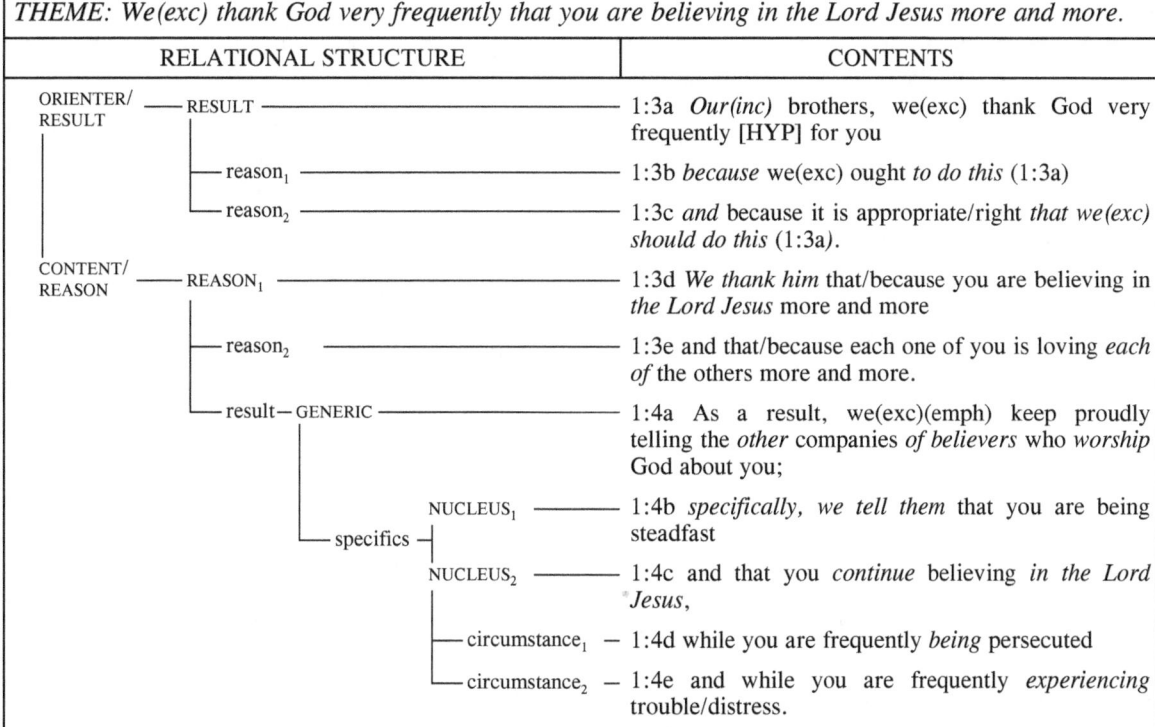

RELATIONAL STRUCTURE	CONTENTS
ORIENTER/RESULT — RESULT	1:3a *Our(inc)* brothers, we(exc) thank God very frequently [HYP] for you
— reason₁	1:3b *because* we(exc) ought *to do this* (1:3a)
— reason₂	1:3c *and because it is appropriate/right that we(exc) should do this* (1:3a).
CONTENT/REASON — REASON₁	1:3d *We thank him* that/because you are believing in *the Lord Jesus* more and more
— reason₂	1:3e and that/because each one of you is loving *each of* the others more and more.
— result — GENERIC	1:4a As a result, we(exc)(emph) keep proudly telling the *other* companies *of believers* who *worship* God about you;
— specifics — NUCLEUS₁	1:4b *specifically, we tell them* that you are being steadfast
NUCLEUS₂	1:4c and that you *continue* believing *in the Lord Jesus*,
— circumstance₁	1:4d while you are frequently *being* persecuted
— circumstance₂	1:4e and while you are frequently *experiencing* trouble/distress.

NOTES

1:3a–b Our(inc) brothers, we(exc) thank God very frequently [HYP] for you *because* we(exc) ought *to do this* (1:3a) The Greek literally has "we thank God always (πάντοτε)," but this is regarded as hyperbolic here and is represented in the display by "very frequently." But it may well be an acceptable hyperbole in other languages than Greek.

A more difficult question is how to handle the Greek verbal phrase εὐχαριστεῖν ὀφείλομεν 'we ought to thank'. Translated literally in this way into English it tends to give the impression that thanking God was something Paul, Silas, and Timothy recognized that they should be doing, but were not actually doing yet.

But the whole context makes it clear that Paul and his colleagues were most grateful to God for the very encouraging progress of the Thessalonian believers. They were actually expressing their thanks to God at this point. Hence, it reflects the semantic structure more accurately and clearly if the obligation expressed is represented by a separate proposition; this is 1:3b. It is widely suggested by the commentators that ὀφείλομεν 'we ought' refers to an *internal* conviction, a subjective oughtness, arising from the fact that these were converts won through the work of Paul and his colleagues, so that they had a special personal interest in thanking God for them and their progress.

However, it is not altogether obvious what the relation between 1:3a and 3b should be. The most likely is that of (subjective) reason—because they were so closely involved with the Thessalonian church, they were constrained to thank God for them.

Dr. John Werner, making use of Aus (1973), suggests that the best way to understand "we ought to thank God" is to see it as language drawn from forms of Jewish worship, and hence "we" as being "we(inc)" rather than the usual we(exc)" of the body introductions in other Pauline letters. Seen this way, it is a sort of exhortation to the effect "we(exc) and you should thank God," and the following καθὼς ἄξιόν ἐστιν 'just as it is fitting/appropriate' (see the notes on 1:3c below) underscores 'that it is always appropriate, in every circumstance, to thank God. In the context, it is seen as particularly appropriate because of the behavior of the Thessalonians in the midst of persecution (many of Aus's examples are found in the context of persecution).

The most obvious problem with this interesting suggestion is that it is saying that the Thessalonian believers should be thanking God for their own faith and love. Werner's answer to this problem is that Paul (as always) is thinking of these as gifts of God, and so they would not be patting themselves on the back, but simply thanking God for his goodness to them.

Werner also suggests that the αὐτοὺς ἡμᾶς 'we ourselves' of 1:4 is a return to we(exc)—only Paul and his colleagues were "boasting" about the Thessalonians.

If this exegesis is followed, it could be expressed in propositions as follows:

(1:3a) We(inc) should thank God very frequently for you,
(1:3b) since it is appropriate/right *that we(inc) should do this (1:3a).*

Constituent 1:3b would be grounds for 1:3a, and there would be no 1:3c.

1:3c *and* because it is appropriate/right *that we(exc) should do this* (1:3a). On first impressions, there is no obvious difference in meaning between we ought" and "it is right/fitting/appropriate" (ἄξιον). The difference is considered to be that this second statement refers to the situation itself, apart from the personal involvement and interest of Paul and the others; the nature of the situation was such that it called for thanksgiving. Proposition 1:3c thus provides a second reason (an "objective" one) for the thanksgiving expressed in 1:3a.

1:3d *We thank him* that/because you are believing in *the Lord Jesus* more and more This proposition is formally marked as a content/reason, being introduced by ὅτι, which commonly signals either of these two relations; there is a formal ambiguity between reason and content at this point. But, in any case, the semantic distinction is not great in this context, nor especially important. "The faith" (ἡ πίστις) is an abstract noun referring to the event of believing or trusting, and since it is collocated with a present tense verb, is understood as referring to the present state of the Thessalonians' faith. No object of the faith is mentioned, but since, in the epistles of the New Testament, saving faith is directed to the Lord Jesus, this is supplied as implicit information here.

The Greek makes use of a dead figure "growing," intensified by the prefix ὑπέρ to "growing very much." The nonfigurative equivalent used in the display is "more and more," and an appropriate way, figurative or nonfigurative, to express the growth of faith, needs to be found for the translation.

1:3e and that/because each one of you is loving *each of* the others more and more. This proposition gives the second content/ reason for the thanksgiving. Again, an abstract noun, love (ἡ ἀγάπη), is used, and collocated with another dead figure "increasing," "becoming greater." In the display, this is represented by the same nonfigurative form "more and more."

Note the emphatic construction "of each one of you all," rather than just "of you."

1:4a As a result, we(exc)(emph) keep proudly telling the *other* companies *of believers* who *worship* God about you; Paul reinforces the two content/reasons by adding a result which gives further information about the character of the Thessalonian believers. In normal English, this Greek construction corresponds to saying (broadly), "your faith and love have grown so much that we are boasting about you!"

The verb, commonly translated "to boast" in English versions, has two focal components—"to speak (or write)," and "to do so with pride." Hence, the display uses "we keep proudly telling," the telling being either by word of mouth or when writing to other churches. (For written examples of such "boasting," see 2 Cor. 8:1-4; 9:2.)

Although there is a textual choice of word order between ἡμᾶς αὐτούς and αὐτοὺς ἡμᾶς, both meaning "we ourselves" in this verse, all are agreed that with either order "we" is being emphasized. But there is no general agreement as to what precise kind of emphasis is being given. Some suggest "we, as well as others," but no others are mentioned (or implied), and it seems likely that this would require the Greek καὶ ἡμᾶς, 'and we, we also'. Others suggest it is a contrastive construction, but there is no obvious contrast in the context. Perhaps the best explanation is that it expressed unexpectedness, i.e., Paul and his colleagues did not generally boast about the results of their own work, but in these circumstances, they did so. It hardly needs to be added that the motive for this boasting was not personal pride, but God's glory and the encouragement of other believers, especially those who were also being persecuted.

"The *other* companies *of believers* which *worship* God" is an attempt to represent the rather unusual (genitive) construction "the churches of God." The word translated "church" (ἐκκλησία) has already been discussed in connection with proposition 1:1a earlier. There it was represented by "the company *of God's people*" since in a number of epistles the broad equivalent "saints" (= God's people) is used to refer to the recipients.

But the genitive construction here, "churches of God" makes that representation rather awkward, so "believers" is used here, rather than "God's people." "Of God" is probably best understood as meaning "worshiping God," but "belonging to God" would be a common use of the genitive construction. Note the implied "the other," since the Thessalonian believers also constituted a "church of God."

1:4b *specifically, we tell them* that you are being steadfast In this proposition, and the following one, Paul spells out what it was specifically about the Thessalonian Christians that caused him to "boast" about them.

The Greek here is simply τῆς ὑπομονῆς ὑμῶν 'your steadfastness', often translated by "patience" or "endurance." But, as Leon Morris points out, it is a positive, active term, not a passive one, and "steadfastness," while somewhat archaic now, conveys this positive note best in English. It almost invariably collocates with persecutions in the New Testament, as here.

1:4c and that you *continue* believing *in the Lord Jesus*, The Greek underlying this proposition is καὶ πίστεως 'and faith'. The lack of repetition of the article, the preposition, and "your," all of which the preceding reference to steadfastness has, link the faith closely with the steadfastness, but not as closely as a genitive construction would have done (cf. 1 Thess. 1:3). Hence, 1:4b and 4c are treated as conjoined, and not linked by a more specific relation, such as reason.

1:4d–e while you are frequently *being persecuted* and while you are frequently *experiencing* trouble/distress. Again, the Greek uses abstract nouns: διωγμοῖς 'persecutions' and θλίψεσιν 'afflictions'. The former term refers to the active hostility of others towards them as Christians, and in the New Testament has the rather specific sense that "persecutions" has in English. The latter term is more general, referring to the troubles experienced by man in this world—sickness, bereavement, hunger, loss of earthly goods, etc.—regardless of the cause. Probably the best term in English is "troubles." However, in the display, these abstract nouns are represented by verb forms. With "persecutions," this is straightforward in English; with "troubles" it is more difficult, so "while you are experiencing trouble/distress" has been used, since "while you are being troubled/distressed" sounds rather odd here.

The Greek phrase is modified by πᾶσιν 'all', applying to both persecutions" and "troubles." While "all" collocates conveniently with nouns, it does not do so with verbs. It is generally agreed that "all" indicates a lot of persecution and trouble, with perhaps some variations in the form they took (loss of goods, imprisonment, ostracism, etc.). Hence, the adverb "frequently" is used, but a possible alternative would be "in various ways."

Both propositions 1:4d and 4e describe the circumstances in which the Thessalonian believers exhibited the qualities of steadfastness and faith. The question has been raised as to whether the relation between these propositions and the preceding pair is that of concession-contraexpectation, i.e., "even though you are being persecuted...." There are two good reasons against this possibility:

1. The Greek is only in the form of a prepositional phrase, using the preposition ἐν 'in', which is very commonly used for circumstances—it is more likely that a concession would have used a conjunction (especially when following the main verb), or a present participle.
2. Was it contrary to expectation that they would be steadfast in persecution? Surely, this was the normal New Testament expectation, and Paul was only worried that they might not have come up to that expectation.

BOUNDARIES AND COHERENCE

The start of this paragraph coincides with the start of the unit 1:3-12 and of the whole body of the letter (1:3-3:16a), so see the notes on boundaries for these two units. But where does it end? This is not a straightforward issue, as the Greek sentence which starts at 1:3 runs on to 1:10, where there is a fairly obvious break.

It is proposed here that 1:3–10 consists of two paragraphs, the first being 1:3–4. The following are the reasons for this decision:

1. There is a major grammatical break at the end of 1:4, and with it the close-knit relations between the propositions of 1:3–4 come to an end.
2. There is a tail-head link between the end of 1:4, which introduces references to the persecutions being undergone by the Thessalonians, and 1:5, which also speaks of their sufferings.
3. There is a change of topic from thanksgiving for the spiritual progress of the Thessalonians in 1:3–4 to that of God's righteous judgment in 1:5–10. Related to this, there is also a switch from present time to future time.
4. Verses 1:3–12 constitute the introductory part of the body of the letter, and so are characterized by a strong "we(exc)-you" orientation. This orientation is very clear in 1:3–4 and 1:11–12, but in 1:5–10 the references are to "we(inc)" (1:7 and 10), and the pattern of "you" references in 1:5–7 is replaced by "they" references in 1:8–10.

As already noted, 1:3–4 is closely knit together relationally (see the display), and references to "you(pl)" and the spiritual characteristics of the Thessalonians are found throughout. Note, too, the two occurrences of "we(exc)" as subject in 1:3–4, data not found again until 1:11. It is also worth noting that all the verb forms in these two verses are in the present tense.

PROMINENCE AND THEME

This is a typical introductory "thanks" paragraph in Paul's letters, in which a "thanks" performative is followed by the reasons for it, which are, at the same time, the contents of it. The theme, then, in this introductory context consists of the performative together with the most important information given as contents/reason for it. In this case, formally, there are two conjoined contents/reasons—the faith of the Thessalonians, and their love for one another. The faith, however, is considered to be marked as more prominent than the love by:

1. Being referred to again in 1:4 (and also later in 1:10 and 11).
2. Being mentioned first (compare the reverse order in Phlm. 5, where "love" is the more prominent, as is shown by further references to it in Phlm. 7 and 9).
3. By being included in Paul's "boasting" (1:4), whereas the love is not.

Hence, the theme consists, essentially, of 1:3a (the performative) and 1:3d (the most prominent content/reason), the vocative being omitted in the theme statement.

SECTION CONSTITUENT 1:5-10 (Paragraph: conjoined to 1:3-4 and 1:11-12)

THEME: God will judge all people justly. Specifically, he will publicly declare that you are worthy to enter that place where he will rule his people forever.

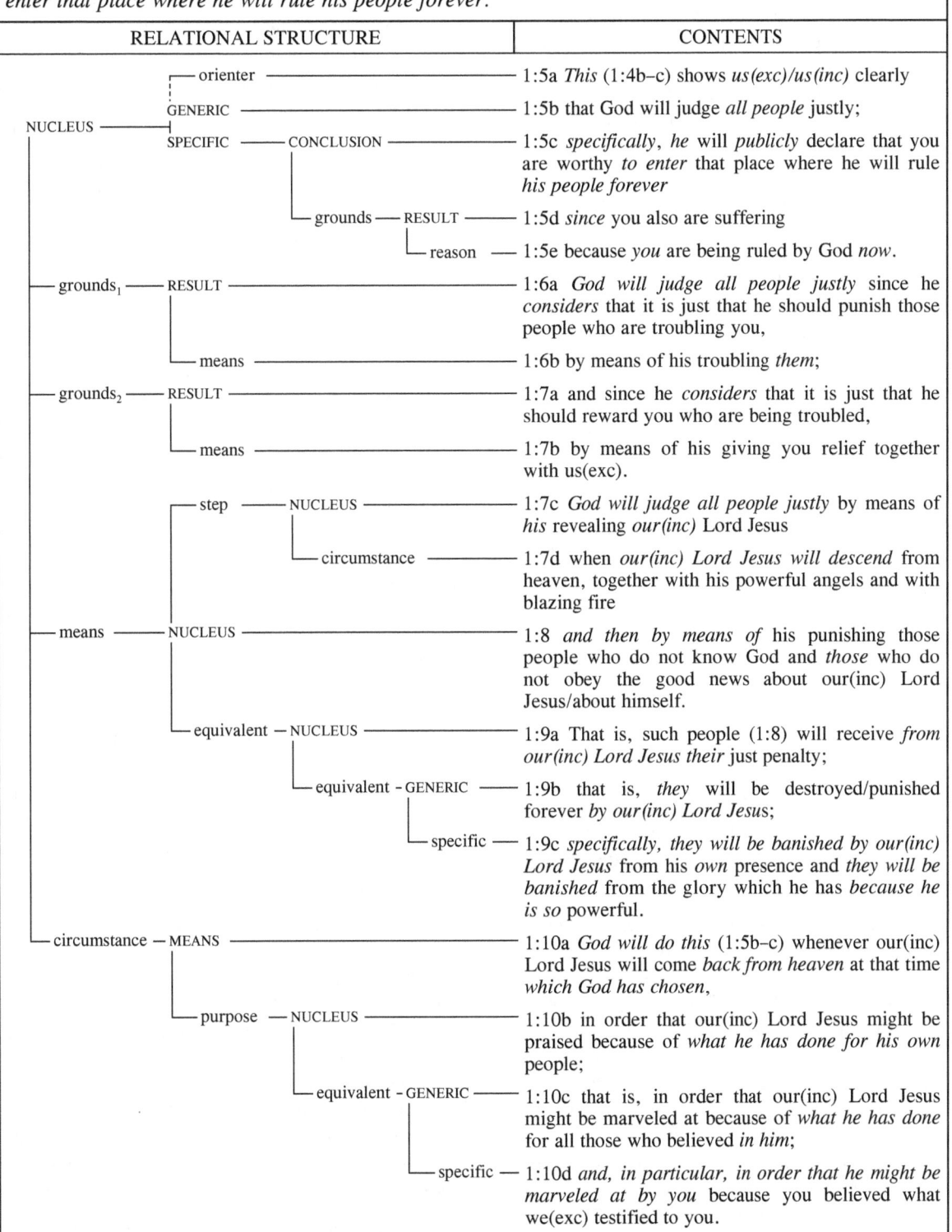

STRUCTURE

This is a long and complex paragraph, so it may be helpful to a translator to outline its structure briefly. Verse 1:5 constitutes the main information of the paragraph—the generic theme (1:5b), the specific theme (1:5c), and the first grounds for these themes (1:5d-e). Verse 1:6 and the first half of 1:7 then support this NUCLEUS cluster by arguing that it is just, in God's estimation, to punish persecutors and reward the persecuted. In the second half of 1:7, the Lord Jesus is introduced, at the time of his return, and 1:8-10 goes on to describe how he will personally put into effect God's righteous judgment. The translator, therefore, may well find it helpful to tackle this long and somewhat difficult paragraph in three parts corresponding to the divisions above.

It may also help to give some idea of the overall logic of this paragraph, as it often is not too clear in the various versions:

> You are suffering for God's Kingdom and are being steadfast in your sufferings—
> Therefore, when Jesus returns, God will declare that you are worthy to enter his eternal Kingdom.
> He will also give you relief from your sufferings, and he will punish those who are persecuting you.

NOTES

From an exegetical standpoint, this is probably the most difficult paragraph in this epistle. Consequently, these notes are on the long side, as it is necessary to justify the decisions reflected in the display in some detail.

1:5a *This* **(1:4b-c) shows** *us(exc)/us(inc)* **clearly**
This proposition represents only one Greek word ἔνδειγμα, variously translated by "proof," "guarantee," "token," "evident indication," "proof positive," "sure sign," "evidence," "plain indication." Quite apart from its meaning (and this is the only occurrence of ἔνδειγμα in the New Testament), there is another important question: What does it relate to?

There is no formal indication of relationship—ἔνδειγμα follows on the preceding word without any overt link. Nevertheless, it is widely agreed that Paul has omitted to use a "this is" or a "which is" connection here. In other words, ἔνδειγμα looks back to what Paul has already said—but to what? The answer to this question is found in what Paul goes on to say in the rest of 1:5 and 1:6-7, which are closely related to 1:5. At the end of 1:5, he refers to their present suffering; in 1:6 he speaks of "those who cause you to suffer"; and in 1:7 "you who are being made to suffer." Hence, it is reasonable to link ἔνδειγμα with what Paul says at the end of 1:4 about the persecutions and sufferings that the Thessalonians were experiencing. However, 1:5-7 also speaks of the recompense or reward that God will give them, so it seems best to refer ἔνδειγμα back to the content of Paul's and his colleagues' "boasting" about the Thessalonians, i.e., to their steadfastness and faith in the midst of persecution. Being persecuted, as such, did not bring the reward; it was their right reaction to it. Paul here is reflecting the Lord's own teaching that "he who has been steadfast to the end, he is the one who will be saved" (Matt. 10:22; 24:13; Mark 13:13). Christians are expected to be steadfast in persecution, and will be abundantly rewarded for so being.

Ἔνδειγμα is yet another example of an abstract noun. Hence, in the display it is represented by a verb "shows." The Greek verb from which this abstract noun is derived is ἐνδείκνυμι, which means "to show, demonstrate (something)." So, the verb "to show" is used, with the modifier "clearly," though "plainly" or "obviously" would also convey the generally agreed sense. The steadfastness and faith of the Thessalonians, in persecution, clearly showed something. But what did it show, and to whom? The first question is answered in the next two propositions. The second is more difficult. This part of section 1:3-12 has many references to "you" (Thessalonians)—eight overt references in 1:4-7; and as Paul's purpose here is to encourage and comfort them in their sufferings, it seems clear that it was (or should have been) an ἔνδειγμα to the Thessalonians themselves. But, since Paul and his colleagues were aware of the situation, and boasted about it to others, they obviously saw clearly what conclusions to draw. Hence, the implicit object of "to show" is given as "us(exc)/us(inc)," depending on whether the Thessalonians are considered to be included or not.

1:5b that God will judge *all people* **justly;** The Greek here is τῆς δικαίας κρίσεως τοῦ θεοῦ 'the righteous judgment of God', equivalent to the propositional form "God will judge justly." The future tense is used because the following verses all speak about the final (future) judgment when the Lord Jesus is revealed. But who is to be judged? As mentioned above, these verses are heavily "you" oriented, and, in particular, the next clause, which is closely related to this one, speaks of God's judgment of the Thessalonians. However, although 1:4–7 is "you" oriented, in 1:6 and 1:8–9 Paul talks more generally of the wicked and the righteous. Further, this phrase "the righteous judgment of God" is the generic theme of the whole paragraph, so while "you" is more appropriate to the immediate context, in the broader context "*all* people" is more appropriate. Since "all people" includes "you," the former is given as the implicit object of "will judge" in the generic part of the theme statement.

This phrase is linked by the genitive construction to ἔνδειγμα, and gives the content of the "showing," i.e., it states, in generic form, what is clearly shown. Hence, 1:5a is the orienter, 1:5b the content it introduces.

1:5c *specifically*, he will *publicly* declare that you are worthy *to enter* that place where he will rule *his people forever* The verb used in the Greek clause is the infinitive καταξιωθῆναι and means "to consider worthy." It is one of the cluster of words in the semantic area of judgment used by Paul here, and since the final judgment is a public affair (as 1:5b implies, as well as 1:8-10), the propositional equivalent has been given as "*publicly* declare...worthy." God's suffering people will be publicly vindicated by the ultimate Judge himself. The verb is passive, but the whole context (1:4-6) is clearly "God" oriented, so God is the one who declares, as in 1:5b. The idea of "worthy" in the verb is "suitable, appropriate, fit" by reason of character and behavior; in this context, their endurance and faith when persecuted.

The believers at Thessalonica are to be declared worthy of "the kingdom of God." This is a common expression in the gospels. Here, in the overall context of the final judgment, the kingdom of God is referred to in its eternal form, the reward and inheritance of God's people. Hence, the display refers to "that place where God will rule *his people forever*." However, "worthy of that place" is a somewhat obscure genitive for a propositional display, so the connection has been made clear by the addition of the implicit information "to enter." God's declaration is that they are the people who will be members or citizens of his eternal kingdom.

There is considerable discussion in the commentaries on the relation between 1:5c and 5b. The Greek is εἰς τό followed by an (aorist) infinitive, and this construction most commonly indicates the relation of purpose, though result is also found. However, it is somewhat unnatural to say "God will judge you in order to declare you worthy"—rather, the declaration is the judgment, a relationship suggested by a minority of the commentators (e.g., Lünemann, Best). Of course, this is also the result of the judgment—there is no real distinction in this context. Hence, 1:5c is analyzed as a more specific statement than that given in 1:5b, but it could be that in some languages, as in Greek, this would be formally expressed as a result.

1:5d–e *since* you also are suffering because *you* are being ruled by God *now*. Paul now "tags on" another reference to their sufferings by means of a relative clause, thus keeping the general context clear, but backgrounded. The Greek is ὑπὲρ ἧς καὶ πάσχετε 'on behalf of which (i.e., the kingdom of God) you are also suffering'. This is essentially a description of the Thessalonians' present state "you are suffering," together with a reason for it, namely, "the kingdom of God." Since their suffering is present, it seems reasonable to regard their relationship to the kingdom as present also, so this is represented by "you are being ruled by God *now*." (There is an implicit contrast between present suffering in connection with God's kingdom and future glory in connection with it, as elsewhere in the New Testament.)

One general question still needs discussion in connection with 1:5, and it is best discussed at the end of 1:5 after the details have been worked out. This question is: In what sense could Paul say that the steadfastness and faith of the Thessalonian Christians under persecution showed plainly that God will act righteously when he declares them worthy of his kingdom? The best answer would seem to be that (a) their being persecuted for being Christians (1:5d–e) and (b) their appropriate behavior in these circumstances showed that they were truly God's own people, righteous in character, and trusting in him. And it is to such people—those who have shown themselves worthy by their deeds—that God's kingdom in its final form is open. This is not salvation by works, but it is the works that prove the reality of a professed faith, as everywhere in the New Testament. Further, the New Testament makes it clear that God's judgment is based on works, i.e., overt evidence, and the Thessalonian believers were showing the appropriate sort of works for a favorable judgment.

1:6a-b *God will judge all people justly* **since he** *considers* **that it is just that he should punish those people who are troubling you, by means of his troubling** *them*; Paul now, as so often in his epistles, supports his main assertion with grounds for it. Propositions 1:6a and 6b give the first ground; propositions 1:7a and 7b give the conjoined second ground. In the display, these grounds are linked to 1:5b-e since Paul discusses the judgment of both persecutors and persecuted. Even so, what he says is still clearly "you"-oriented.

These two grounds are introduced by the conjunction εἴπερ, which is rather rare, being used only by Paul in the New Testament, and only five other times by him (Rom. 3:30; 8:9,17; 1 Cor. 8:5; 15:15). This form would appear to indicate doubt or uncertainty (since εἰ means "if") but it is widely agreed that here it presents a certain assumption, i.e., "assuming (for argument's sake) what we all know to be true." Since a known fact (about God's character) is appealed to here, it is better to call it grounds, rather than condition.

The phrase that follows the conjunction εἴπερ is δίκαιον παρὰ θεῷ 'a righteous-thing with God', "righteous" translating the same Greek adjective δίκαιος as was used at the beginning of 1:5 in connection with God's judgment. Much the same idea is being expressed here—"a righteous-thing with God" meaning "in his estimation," or "by his standards." What is regarded as righteous (or "just") by God is spelled out in the rest of 1:6 and the first part of 1:7. It is essentially that evil should be appropriately punished, and righteousness rewarded.

The first righteous act is ἀνταποδοῦναι τοῖς θλίβουσιν ὑμᾶς θλῖψιν 'to give back (in full), to those who are afflicting you, affliction'; that is to say, "to make the punishment fit the crime." Jews and Gentiles in Thessalonica were persecuting the Christians, causing them distress. In response (which is the force of the Greek word ἀνταποδοῦναι, used here), God will cause them distress in his judgment.

Proposition 1:6b separates out the actual punishment as a means: "by means of his troubling *them*." It should be noted, however, that neither form of 1:6a and 6b does justice to the components of the Greek verb ἀνταποδίδωμι, which conveys the idea "give back in exchange in full." Here, the appropriateness of God's dealings with the persecutors is only carried implicitly by the use of the same lexical items in 1:6a and 6b.

1:7a and since he *considers* **that it is just that he should reward you who are being troubled,** It will be seen that proposition 1:7a overlaps considerably with 1:6a in content. The only difference is that persecutors are being punished in 1:6a; in 1:7a, the persecuted are being rewarded, or recompensed.

In the Greek, the same verb ἀνταποδίδωμι underlies this proposition (the verb is implicit in the Greek, but is clearly implied by the use of καί 'and', and by the fact that parallel constructions are dependent on it—a dative phrase and an accusative phrase). However, it is represented in the display by "reward," since here it is the persecuted Thessalonians to whom the verb applies. "Recompense," however, is probably nearest the sense, since it carries something of the idea of the "reward fitting the suffering," the "giving back in exchange in full."

1:7b by means of his giving you relief together with us(exc). This is a means proposition parallel with 1:6c. "Relief" seems the best English word to convey the idea of the Greek ἄνεσιν (usually translated "rest") in this context. It refers to the absence of suffering, trouble, distress, i.e., the converse of what the Thessalonians were currently experiencing.

1:7c *God will judge all people justly* **by means of** *his* **revealing** *our(inc)* **Lord Jesus** As pointed out in the discussion of the structure of this passage, the end of 1:7 introduces the Lord Jesus for the first time in the body of this epistle, i.e., since the formal opening salutation in 1:1-2. He now becomes the agent in the second half of this paragraph, replacing God the Father as agent.

Again, an abstract noun is used, ἀποκαλύψει 'revelation/revealing'. It has the sense of revealing what was hidden, in this case the visible presence of the Lord Jesus, now hidden from sight in heaven. It is used in connection with the Lord's return also in 1 Cor. 1:7; 1 Pet. 1:7, 13; 4:13; and the cognate verb ἀποκαλύπτω is used in Luke 17:30; compare also Rom. 8:18, 19; 1 Cor. 3:12, 13; 1 Pet. 1:5; 5:1, where events connected with "the day" (see 1:10) are spoken of as "revealed." The question arises as to whether God (the Father) reveals Jesus, or Jesus reveals himself. The former is probably better (cf. the passive in Luke 17:30, and also here in 1:10). At God's chosen time, he is revealed for all to see. But the reflexive "he reveals himself" is acceptable.

Two difficult questions arise in connection with the phrase ἐν τῇ ἀποκαλύψει 'in the revelation'. What does it relate back to and what is the semantic relation?

1. In 1:6 and the first half of 1:7, Paul has argued that God will punish persecutors and reward the persecuted and that it is just and fair that he should do so. It seems something of a sudden jump to then refer to an actual event in close connection with an argument. Hence, it seems more logical to connect 1:7c-d back to the generic statement "God will judge all people justly" (1:5b), rather than to add it in as part of the argument.

2. The preposition ἐν commonly signals circumstances or means, but it is not at all obvious which is preferable here. Both make good sense: it is *when* the Lord Jesus is revealed that God's righteous judgment is put into effect; and it is also *by means of* his appearing and judging—he is the appointed judge. It is possible that the answer hinges on a fine point of Greek grammar and semantics. After referring to the revealing of the Lord Jesus, Paul goes on to say (of him) διδόντος ἐκδίκησιν 'giving vengeance', using a present participle in concord with the noun "Jesus." The other grammatical alternative, common in Paul's letters, would have been to have put ὃς δώσει ἐκδίκησιν 'who will give vengeance'. The relative clause, in Paul's letters, either simply describes the person or thing referred to, or, quite commonly, makes a transition to a new, though closely related, semantic topic and unit. Hence, it could be that Paul did not use a relative clause here because the same topic of God's righteous judgment is being continued. Also, the use of διδόντος 'giving' links this event very closely to the ἀποκαλύψει 'revealing', whereas the relative clause would tend to separate it off.

Hence, since ἐν commonly signals means, and since Jesus is the appointed judge, and since the participle διδόντος 'giving' is used, preference is given to the relation of means. But the distinction is a fine one (and the argument is only plausible rather than conclusive), so the relation of circumstance is a well-accepted alternative here.

1:7d when *our(inc) Lord Jesus will descend from heaven, together with his powerful angels and with blazing fire* In the original, three prepositional phrases follow the abstract noun ἀποκαλύψει, which describe the place Jesus comes from, who accompanies him, and the physical circumstances. Since the first of these carries the implicit idea of movement, the prepositional phrases have been handled as a separate proposition (1:7d).

"To descend" seems the most appropriate verb here, though, more precisely expressed, this could be "when he comes out from heaven, and descends." It could also be argued, however, that only the first of these movements is implied here, the other being taught elsewhere, e.g., in 1 Thess. 4:16. In that verse, however, the verb "he will descend" is followed by exactly the same prepositional phrase as here, so "descends" seems a reasonable inference, if a verb of motion has to be supplied.

There is a complex genitive construction underlying the next phrase—μετ' ἀγγέλων δυνάμεως αὐτοῦ 'with angels-of-power of-him'. There is considerable discussion in the commentaries as to whether the αὐτοῦ 'of-him' refers to the power or to the angels, i.e., is it "his angels of power" or "angels of his power"? Since both are certainly true, that is, since the angels belong to him as his creatures and servants, and since he has given them power, it is not an important choice. The first view is shown in the display; the second view, generally more popular with commentators, would lead to the propositional form "accompanied by angels, to whom he had given power," or something equivalent.

There are three questions that arise in connection with the third phrase:

1. The first is a textual one—did the original read "in a flame of fire" or "in a fire of flame"? There is little agreement as to which is the better text, but fortunately semantically there seems little, if any, distinction in meaning. Regardless of the text followed, almost all versions translate by "in flaming fire" or "in blazing fire," i.e., the concept of "fire" is intensified to mean a very hot fire.

2. Does this phrase belong with 1:7d or is it part of 1:8? Two arguments favor linking it with 1:7d:
   a. It gives a rather unusual word order, with an initial prepositional phrase preceding a participle, if it is linked with 1:8. This is not impossible, but it would give considerable prominence to the blazing fire.
   b. Collocationally, it seems more appropriate as a description of the revelation of Jesus from heaven, rather than the act of judgment described in 1:8.

   Hence, in the display, it is attached to 1:7, and 1:8 is regarded as beginning with the participle διδόντος 'giving'. (This statement arises because there is some variation as to where 1:8 is considered to begin.)
3. So far as the translator is concerned, is it to be considered a reference to literal fire, or is it metaphorical for, say, the presence of God himself? The answer would seem to be that it is both, as is often the case in the Old Testament, for example, when God made a covenant with Abraham (Gen. 15:17), or the pillar of fire at the time of the exodus, or the fire and lightning on Mount Sinai, or Ezekiel's vision of God (Ezek. 1:4, 5, 13, 14); cf. also the "tongues as of fire" on the Day of Pentecost. Hence, it can be plausibly argued that "fire" is a symbol (see Beekman and Callow 1974:136 for a brief discussion of symbols) used in both the Old Testament and the New Testament and, therefore, should be retained literally in a translation.

1:8 *and then by means of* **his punishing those people who do not know God and** *those* **who do not obey the good news about our(inc) Lord Jesus/about himself.** Having reached the conclusion that 1:7d is the means by which God judges everyone righteously, the question is then raised as to what relation 1:8 has to 1:7d. It is introduced by διδόντος 'giving', a present participle referring back to the Lord Jesus in 1:7c and d. This yields the sequence "by the revelation of the Lord Jesus...giving vengeance." The two events of revealing and judging are very closely tied together, and both are "governed" by the ἐν 'by', signaling means. Hence, the "exacting vengeance" is analyzed as means also, and the relation between the two events of "revealing" and "exacting vengeance" is considered to be a step-goal relation. That is to say, they are considered to be in sequence (however long or short the time interval), and the first is necessary if the second is to take place. Clearly, in this context, the second event, "exacting vengeance," is the more prominent of the two, and so is labeled NUCLEUS.

The two opening Greek words διδόντος ἐκδίκησιν 'giving vengeance' are generally translated as "taking/exacting vengeance." It seems very likely that the expression, and the ideas behind it, come from the Old Testament. This precise collocation "give vengeance" is used in Ezek. 25:14. A study of the Hebrew root (*nqm*), frequently translated by ἐκδίκησις and ἐκδικέω in the Septuagint, reveals the following factors in connection with it:

1. It is God, often *YHWH*, who does it; it is not man's business. The Edomites and the Philistines are rebuked in Ezek. 25:12 and 15 for taking vengeance into their own hands. However, sometimes God calls on human agents to act on his behalf (as in Ps. 149:7 and Jer. 50:15).
2. God exacts vengeance on those who are wicked—usually his and his people's enemies (e.g., Babylon; see Isa. 47:3 and Jer. 50:15,28). But it can also be on the wicked and rebellious among the Israelites themselves (as in Ezek. 24:8).
3. God exacts vengeance righteously—it is one part of his work as the perfectly righteous judge; see, for example, Jer. 11:20, which reads, "you who judge righteously and test the heart and mind, let me see your vengeance on them."
4. There is also the component, closely related to point 3, that the wicked get exactly what they deserve. Jeremiah (in 51:6) says, "It is time for the Lord's vengeance; he will pay her what she deserves."

Although the verb ἐκδικέω and the corresponding noun ἐκδίκησις are not common in the New Testament (the former is used five times, and the latter nine), most of the above components, or collocations, are clearly apparent. It is always those who are wicked on whom vengeance is exacted, whether the stubborn Jews (Luke 21:22; cf. also the context of Heb. 10:30) or disobedient Christians (2 Cor. 10:6) or the wicked in general (1 Pet. 2:14; Rev. 19:2). It is linked with God's righteousness as in the present passage; see also Rev. 6:10, where a call to God to avenge addresses him as "the holy and true one." The component of "paying back" has already been expressed in the present passage with ἀνταποδίδωμι in 1:6.

The biggest difference is in the expressed agents of the vengeance. God is clearly the agent in Luke 18:7, 8; 21:22; Rom. 12:19 (a quote from the Old Testament); Heb. 10:30 (the same quote); Rev. 6:10 and 19:2. But in Luke 18:3 and 5 it is a judge; in Acts 7:24 it is Moses; in 2 Cor. 7:11 it is the Corinthians themselves; in 2 Cor. 10:6 it is Paul; and in 1 Pet. 2:14 it is the civil authorities. (In the present passage it is the Lord Jesus.) However, it is clear from the passage in Peter that God has given authority to the civil authorities to act, as it were, on his behalf in this matter, and this explains each of the other cases—the judge, Moses (conscious of the divine call), Paul (with his apostolic authority), and the Corinthians (with the authority given to the local church to deal with flagrant sin).

In this proposition, then, the meaning of "giving vengeance" is that of punishing those who have acted wickedly exactly as they deserve.

The rest of the proposition, in fact, describes the wicked who are being punished. Some commentators deduce from the repetition of the article with the two phrases that two different classes of evil people are being described—Gentiles, described as "those who do not know God" (in distinction from the Jews; see 1 Thess. 4:5; and Rom. 1:28; Gal. 4:8; Eph. 2:12), and Jews, described as "those who have rejected the gospel" (cf. Rom. 10:3, 16, 21); or alternatively, the heathen, described as "those who do not know God," and Jews and Gentiles who have rejected the gospel. Certainly, both groups would be present in Thessalonica. Others, however, take it as a twofold description of those judged, in their attitude to God (the Father) and to the Lord Jesus. It is hard to know which view is preferable. If the latter view is followed, "those who do not know God" is generally taken to mean "those who refuse to know God," i.e., as a deliberate turning away from God as revealed in the gospel, rather than a description of heathen ignorance. And "do not obey the gospel" is regarded as equivalent to "reject the gospel." So far as the translator is concerned, there is no need, if either of the first views is followed, to make explicit reference to Gentiles and Jews.

The final phrase in this verse is another example of the genitive construction: τῷ εὐαγγελίῳ τοῦ κυρίου ἡμῶν Ἰησοῦ 'the gospel of the Lord of us, Jesus'. Here it is much better to understand this construction as meaning "the gospel which tells about our Lord Jesus" rather than "the gospel which came from our Lord Jesus." He is the great subject matter of the gospel; without him, and all that he has done, there is no gospel.

1:9a That is, such people (1:8) will receive *from our(inc) Lord Jesus their* just penalty; The phrase "such people" reflects the Greek relative οἵτινες, and refers to all who do not know God and reject the gospel.

This proposition is the reciprocal of 1:8. There the Lord Jesus is described as inflicting a just and merited punishment. Here, those who are punished are described as receiving their just penalty. Proposition 1:8 is from the standpoint of the judge; 1:9a from the standpoint of those judged. The collocation is a common Greek legal one. As the reciprocal, its relation to 1:8 is that of equivalence.

1:9b that is, *they* will be destroyed/punished forever *by our(inc) Lord Jesus*; This proposition gives a brief description of what that just penalty is, literally, "eternal destruction" (ὄλεθρον αἰώνιον). Αἰώνιον 'eternal' is the same word as that used in the phrase "eternal life," and is the "second death" referred to in the book of Revelation. "Destroy" is further explained in the following propositions as eternal separation from God, not annihilation, and lexical choices should be avoided that would imply the latter.

This proposition is analyzed as equivalent to 1:9a, in that it explains what the "just penalty" is. Alternatively, it could be regarded as a more specific description of the just penalty. In either case, it is a restatement relation, signaled by an appositional construction in the Greek.

1:9c *specifically, they will be banished by our(inc) Lord Jesus* from his *own* presence and *they will be banished* from the glory which he has *because he is so* powerful. By means of prepositional phrases Paul now spells out what "eternal destruction" means in more detail; hence, this proposition is analyzed as a specific of the preceding generic proposition.

The first of the two prepositional phrases is ἀπὸ προσώπου τοῦ κυρίου 'from face of the Lord'. The word προσώπου 'face' here is an idiomatic way of referring to the Lord's presence; and ἀπό 'from' or 'away from', since it is collocated with, in effect, a location "where the Lord is," is an abbreviated way of saying "banished/removed from." In other words, eternal life is to know God, and to spend eternity in his presence; the opposite, for those who do not know God, is eternal destruction, and is to be banished from his presence forever. Τοῦ κυρίου 'the Lord' is understood as referring to the Lord Jesus, as in the preceding verse, and so, if this proposition is expressed in an active form with the Lord Jesus as agent of the banishing, then it will be necessary to give the equivalent of "from his own presence."

The second prepositional phrase ἀπὸ τῆς δόξης τῆς ἰσχύος αὐτοῦ 'from the glory of the might of him' is more difficult exegetically. Αὐτοῦ 'him, is still referring to the Lord Jesus, and the whole phrase is not referring to another, distinct punishment, but refers to the same banishment, but from a different perspective. The question is how to understand the genitive construction "the glory of the might of him," i.e., in particular, how are δόξης 'glory' and ἰσχύος 'might' to be related to each other? Since, in this context, the presence of the Lord is also the presence of his glory, it seems preferable to take "glory" as the principal description. "Mighty glory," a possible collocation, does not make a lot of sense. Since the Lord Jesus is demonstrating his supreme power by acting as the righteous judge of all men, probably the best understanding is along the lines of "the glory of him who has (such) mighty power," or "of him who is so powerful." However, since "presence" and "glory" are so closely connected, a possible translation would be: "he will banish them from his own glorious presence, which he has because he is so powerful."

1:10a God will do this (1:5b–c) whenever our(inc) Lord Jesus will come back from heaven at that time which God has chosen, This proposition gives the circumstances in which the above judgment of the wicked will take place. But to what previous statement(s) does it relate? Two observations would indicate that it should be related back to the NUCLEUS propositional cluster (1:5b–e) of this paragraph.

1. The fact that a finite verb form (ἔλθῃ 'he (may) come') is used (the first since 1:6, apart from the relative clause in 1:9) probably indicates that 1:10 is not just attached to the end of 1:9 (itself a relative clause).

2. Verse 1:10 returns to the topic of the righteous, which can be related more readily to the NUCLEUS cluster than to any subsequent material.

Hence, 1:10, of which 1:19a is the main proposition, is considered to be giving the circumstances of 1:5b–e.

The Greek is ὅταν ἔλθῃ 'whenever he may come', i.e., referring to an event which will take place at an unknown time in the future; the event is certain, the time is not. The Greek verb ἔρχομαι is the usual verb meaning "to come," i.e., move towards the speaker. In English, we commonly refer to this event as Jesus "returning" or "coming back," since he has been here once already, but this was evidently not necessary in Greek. If a location is required with a verb of motion, it should be "from heaven" as in 1:7. In fact, this proposition is an abbreviated reference back to the fuller statement in 1:7d.

In the Greek, 1:10 finishes with the words ἐν τῇ ἡμέρᾳ ἐκείνῃ 'on that day'. They follow a parenthetical clause (see 1:10d), and they refer again to the time of the events of 1:10. Since 1:10a is the main proposition in this verse, and since "on that day" refers to 1:10a–c, it is put as a phrase into 1:10a, as is done in some of the versions. It could be argued that ἐν τῇ ἡμέρᾳ ἐκείνῃ corresponds to and refers to ἐν τῇ ἀποκαλύψει τοῦ κυρίου Ἰησοῦ 'in the revealing of the Lord Jesus' (1:7), forming a sandwich structure for this material in which prominence is given to the Lord Jesus. In the Greek, this is made more obvious by placing it sentence final; but semantically, it defines the time of the coming in 1:10a. The word ἡμέρα 'day' may need to be translated by "time" in some languages, since it is not a twenty-four-hour period of time that is in view. "On that day" is a common Old Testament phrase for the time when God acts decisively (and finally) in judgment on his enemies and in blessing on his people. To make clearer its special sense, it may be necessary to add "that God has chosen/appointed."

1:10b–c in order that our(inc) Lord Jesus might be praised because of what he has done for his own people; that is, in order that our(inc) Lord Jesus might be marveled at because of what he has done for all those who believed in him; There are other purposes in the return of the Lord Jesus than that of punishing the wicked, and these are now given in 1:10b–d.

The verbal form here is generally translated by "to be glorified"; the verb is a compound, ἐνδοξάζω, of the usual form δοξάζω 'glorify'. In the New Testament it used only here and below in 1:12. Since the verb is also followed by an ἐν phrase (ἐν τοῖς ἁγίοις αὐτοῦ 'in his saints'), there is some uncertainty as to how the verb and the phrase are to be related. The two main alternatives are:

1. Ἐν signals the agent of the passive action referred to by the verb, so that it is his saints who glorify Jesus.
2. Ἐν means more strictly "in"; that is to say, Jesus' glory is seen "in" his transformed and glorified saints, and he will therefore receive glory (from unspecified beings) for his glory as seen in his people. This sense is probably best conveyed by saying "because of his *own* people," where this represents "because of what he has done for his *own* people."

A second parallel purpose is given with broadly synonymous vocabulary items. The verb ἐνδοξασθῆναι 'to be glorified' is replaced by θαυμασθῆναι 'to be marveled at', and τοῖς ἁγίοις 'his saints' by πᾶσιν τοῖς πιστεύσασιν 'all those who believed'. In the phrase "those who believed" the past (aorist) tense is used because their believing took place before the events spoken of here. The choice which was made for the preceding proposition regarding the handling of the "in" should be followed in this proposition also, since they are so strongly parallel.

1:10d *and, in particular, in order that he might be marveled at by you* because you believed what we(exc) testified to you. All the commentators are agreed that the clause which represents this proposition is parenthetical. Paul has just referred to "all those who believed," and he hastens to reassure the Thessalonians that he regards them as among that group. Hence, it stands as a specific "you who believed" in relation to the generic "all who believed."

The genitive phrase (with abstract noun) τὸ μαρτύριον ἡμῶν 'the testimony of us' refers to the testimony or witness of Paul, Timothy, and Silas when they arrived in Thessalonica and preached the gospel there, i.e., it represents "what we testified." The testimony was directed "to you" (ἐφ' ὑμᾶς) and the context, plus, perhaps, the use of the preposition ἐπί indicates that that witness was believed by the Thessalonians.

BOUNDARIES AND COHERENCE

The arguments for starting a new paragraph with 1:5 have already been presented in connection with 1:3–4. Verse 1:11 is clearly marked as a new start, with a new performative "we pray," a return to the "we-you" orientation, and a change of topic from God's righteous judgment to prayer for the Thessalonians. In addition, there is a tail-head link in that the final clause in 1:10 reintroduces the "we-you" orientation absent from 1:5–9.

Coherence in 1:5–10 is very strong. With the topic being "the righteous judgment of God," there is a considerable vocabulary drawn from the legal sphere, a number of the items sharing the common root *δικ:

δίκαιος 'righteous' (i.e., "just, fair, unbiased" in this context) (5, 6)
κρίσις 'judgment' (i.e., the act of judging) (5)
καταξιόω 'to declare worthy' (of a reward, in this case) (5)
ἀνταποδίδωμι 'to pay back (fully)' (i.e., "to punish/reward as someone deserves") (6)
δίδωμι ἐκδίκησιν 'to exact (give) vengeance' (i.e., "to inflict a justly deserved punishment on the wicked") (8)
δίκην τίνω 'to receive a just penalty' (9)

In addition, God is the explicit or implicit subject of all the verbs in 1:5–6 (other than the relative clause in 1:5) and the Lord Jesus is similarly the subject in 1:8–10, apart from the relative clause in 1:9 and the ὅτι 'because' clause in 1:10. This paragraph, unlike either of the preceding or following paragraphs, is characterized by lexical contrasts (1:6–7, 8–9,10) and by parallel statements linked by καί 'and' (1:6–7, 8, 9, 10).

Grammatically, 1:5–10 is punctuated by the editors of Greek New Testaments as part of one long sentence running from 1:3 to 1:10, the verses being closely linked together by such devices as conjunctions, a concordant participle, and a relative pronoun.

PROMINENCE AND THEME

In spite of being such a coherent paragraph, it is not at all easy to determine the prominence patterns. Proposition 1:5b "God will judge *all people* justly" is analyzed as a generic theme, and all the other propositions can be related to this proposition directly or indirectly. Normally, this would point to 1:5b as being the theme statement for these verses. However, 1:5c is specific in relation to 1:5b, stating what God's just judgment would actually be for the Thessalonians. This more specific statement is regarded as being equally prominent with 1:5b on the grounds that:

1. A single specific proposition is more prominent than the generic proposition to which it is related. In this case, however, the centrality of 1:5b to the whole paragraph indicates that it is not less prominent than 1:5c; hence, they are given equal prominence.
2. The whole section 1:3–12 is the introduction of the body of the letter, and so is essentially we-you oriented, even though 1:5–10 is only partially so, and hence, the "you"-ness of 1:5c makes it prominent in the context of this section. In other words, the purpose of this paragraph is not only to teach the Thessalonians some truths about God's just judgment of all men—it is to apply these truths to them in their persecuted state, so as to encourage them.

Hence, the theme statement is considered to consist of both propositions 1:5b and 5c.

SECTION CONSTITUENT 1:11–12 (Paragraph: Nucleus₂ of 1:3–12)

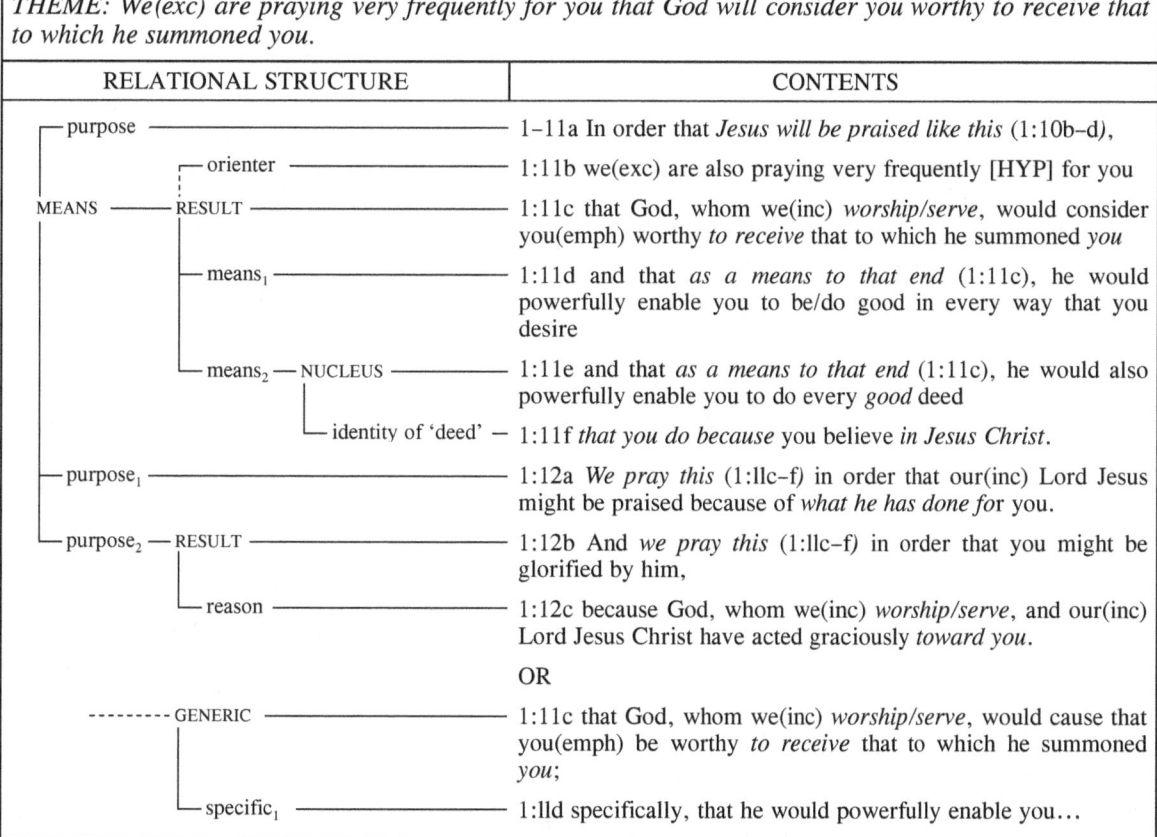

NOTES

1:11a In order that *Jesus will be praised like this* (1:10b-d), The introduction to 1:11–12 is simply εἰς ὅ, which can be understood as meaning "to which end" or "with regard to which" depending on what sense εἰς is understood to have. Since this phrase is attached to a prayer, which is often collocated with purposes; and since the immediately preceding verse has indicated God's purpose that his saving people should glorify Jesus, the εἰς ὅ is regarded as signaling a purpose, and that purpose is the one expressed in propositions 1:10b-d. (It is, in fact, very similar to the purpose expressed in more detail in proposition 1:12a, later in this same paragraph.) The suggestion that εἰς ὅ signals a purpose, but looks forward to the purpose or content of the prayer, is rejected on the grounds that the relative pronoun ὅ always refers back, not forward; εἰς τοῦτο 'to this end' would be needed for a forward reference.

1:11b we(exc) are also praying very frequently [HYP] for you As in 1:3a earlier, πάντοτε 'always' is taken as a hyperbole, with the nonfigurative sense of "very frequently."

The opening εἰς ὅ 'with respect to which' (see discussion above) is followed by καί 'and'. This conjunction regularly links together grammatical units of the same rank—word to word, phrase to phrase, etc. Here it is attached to "we pray" (or the whole of the clause—it makes no essential difference) and the only other grammatical unit of that sort is "we ought to thank" in 1:3. Hence, the καί is understood as indicating that Paul, Silas, and Timothy both thanked God for the Thessalonians and also prayed for them.

1:11c that God, whom we(inc) *worship/serve*, would consider you(emph) worthy *to receive* that to which he summoned *you* The conjunction ἵνα introduces the content of the prayer, using a purpose conjunction, as other languages do.

The pronoun ὑμᾶς 'you(pl)' precedes the verb and so is to be considered highlighted— "it is for you that we are praying" (Friberg 1982:3.1.a).

The Greek phrase ὁ θεὸς ἡμῶν 'the God of us' is propositionalized as "God, whom we(inc) *worship/serve*" as the noun "God" may not be "possessed" in certain languages.

Although "call" is traditionally used in English to translate the verb καλέω and the cognate noun, κλῆσις, used here, since "call" generally means either "to shout to/for" or 'give a name to," the verb "to summon" is used here as, although archaic, it conveys the idea of an authoritative invitation, which may not be turned down, which is the sense of "call" in Paul's writings.

The Greek collocation ἀξιώσῃ τῆς κλήσεως 'count worthy of the calling' presents an interesting exegetical problem. In the other places in the New Testament where the verb ἀξιόω is used (Luke 7:7; Acts 15:38; 28:22; 1 Tim. 5:17; Heb. 3:3; 10:29) all are agreed that it means "to consider worthy," or, in the Acts examples "to consider worthwhile." On the other hand, the noun κλῆσις (and its cognate verb καλέω), when used by Paul, refers to the divine "call" or "summons" which brings those called to faith and salvation. How then could Paul and the others be praying that God would consider the Thessalonians worthy of something that had already happened to them?

Basically, two answers have been proposed to resolve this problem:

1. In this context, which includes teaching on the coming judgment, the final kingdom of God, relief for the persecuted, and glory with Christ, the noun κλῆσις 'call' is to be understood as referring not only to the initial act of calling sinners, but to all that is implied with it—in particular, a godly walk (see Eph. 4:1) and the future glory after this life (cf. Phil. 3:14). It is pointed out by Best that ἐλπίς 'hope', a similar type of noun, clearly refers to "what is hoped for" in Col. 1:5, rather than the activity of hoping. Similarly, πίστις 'faith' can refer both to the activity of believing, and to the content of what is believed (as several times in the pastoral epistles). Hence, one solution is to take the view that κλῆσις 'call' is used in that way here and refers to what Christians are called to, so that it is virtually equivalent to hope in the sense "what is hoped for."

2. The other solution is, in effect, the reverse. It is maintained that κλῆσις 'call' has its usual sense of God's calling the sinner to salvation, and that the verb ἀξιόω means "to cause to be worthy" rather than "to consider to be worthy." Although there are no New Testament instances of this sense, Arndt and Gingrich cite one example from Diognetus, and it certainly makes for a much more straightforward relation to the two following propositions, where Paul is praying for God's work in the life of the believers.

Of these two alternatives, the first is preferred as it makes a relatively slight assumption concerning the sense of κλῆσις 'call'; the second has to assume a sense for ἀξιόω without confirmation in the New Testament. If the second alternative is preferred, then in 1:11c "consider you(emph) worthy" should be altered to "cause that you(emph) be worthy"; and 1:11d and e would be conjoined specifics of 1:11c.

1:11d–f and that *as a means to that end* (1:11c), he would powerfully enable you to be/do good in every way that you desire and that *as a means to that end* (1:11c), he would also powerfully enable you to do every *good* deed *that you do because you believe in Jesus Christ*. The clause representing this proposition is linked by καί 'and' to the preceding clause, so Paul and the others are represented as praying that God would consider the Thessalonians worthy and that....However, what follows the καί 'and' is a prayer for God's work in the lives of the Thessalonians, so that it is not really parallel with the opening prayer (unless the second alternative above is followed). In fact, since God's considering them worthy is closely tied up with the quality of their Christian lives, Paul and the others pray that God will work in them to that end. However, in the propositional form, this is expressed as "and that *as a means to that end* (1:11c)" to try to show the connection between the two halves of the prayer. In other words, Paul and his colleagues are praying two things, the second of which is a means to the answering of the first.

The verb used in the Greek is πληρόω, which is translated variously as "bring to completion," "fulfill, complete," etc. Since it is activities of the Thessalonians which are to be completed by God, semantically this (presumably) does not mean that the Thessalonian believers do, say, 80%, and then God adds the other 20%, which is what "bring to completion" would be understood as meaning in normal English. Hence, in this collocation, πληρόω is understood to mean that God will enable the Thessalonians to fully do, i.e., it is understood in a causative sense.

The grammatical object of the verb is a compound noun phrase, the first part being πᾶσαν εὐδοκίαν ἀγαθωσύνης 'all desire of (moral) goodness'. This is a further example of the genitive construction, and the question arises of how the two parts are related. Also, both nouns are abstract nouns.

First, it should be said that both nouns are taken as referring to the Thessalonians, not to God (cf. the KJV "of his goodness"). It is true that εὐδοκία 'resolve' is used of God, but it is also used of man in Rom. 10:1 and Phil. 1:15. And ἀγαθωσύνη '(moral) goodness' is only used of man (Rom. 15:14; Gal. 5:22; Eph. 5:9). In addition, the parallel ἔργον πίστεως 'work of faith' obviously refers to the Thessalonians.

Secondly, there is the question of what εὐδοκία means when used of human beings. In Rom. 10:1, it refers to Paul's strong desire or longing that his fellow Jews would be saved; in Phil. 1:15 it refers to those who were preaching Christ "out of good will" while Paul was imprisoned, as opposed to those whose motives were bad. So it refers both to a good desire and to good motives. In either case, the idea is incomplete; there is a desire for something, or a motivation towards something good.

Hence, thirdly, it seems preferable to take ἀγαθωσύνης 'goodness' as what was desired. The genitive construction would then mean "you desire that you be/do good." There seems little ground for choosing between the two alternatives "be" and "do," so both are given in the display.

Fourthly, this phrase is preceded by πᾶσαν 'all'. In the display, this concept has to relate to being/doing good, so is represented by "in every way."

The second half of the compound noun phrase is ἔργον πίστεως 'work of faith', another genitive construction, one already used in 1 Thess. 1:3. It is generally agreed that since the two phrases are linked by καί 'and' the opening πᾶσαν 'all' applies to both; hence, "every work of faith." The noun ἔργον 'work' in Paul's writings means "good deeds," the outward acts, as opposed to inner attitudes; and like everything else in the Christian faith, such good deeds are the expression of faith, i.e., they are done because of faith in the Lord Jesus. However, again, this is not easily put into propositional form. Note that 1:11f is an identification, identifying the good deeds as those which they are doing because they believe.

The clause being considered finishes with the prepositional phrase ἐν δυνάμει 'in power', and this phrase modifies the verb πληρώσῃ 'fulfill, complete'. It is Paul's prayer that God would powerfully enable the Thessalonians to live godly lives. An alternative way of regarding ἐν δυνάμει would be as "by (his) power," which could be more suitable for some languages.

1:12a *We pray this* **(1:11c–f) in order that our(inc) Lord Jesus might be praised because of** *what he has done for* **you.** The clause representing this proposition is introduced by the conjunction ὅπως. All are agreed that it signals "purpose" here. The usual ἵνα is not used, the commentators suggest, either because it has just been used to introduce the preceding clauses, and so ὅπως is used for stylistic variation; or, possibly, because the purpose introduced by the ὅπως is grammatically dependent on a ἵνα clause, and introduces a more ultimate purpose.

The wording of this clause is very obviously similar to the wording of the first part of 1:10. The same rare verb ἐνδοξάζω 'to glorify' is used, with essentially the same subject ("the Lord Jesus" in 1:10, "the name of our Lord Jesus" here); and is, in each case, followed by the preposition ἐν 'in' and a reference to believers ("his saints" in 1:10, "you" here). Hence, 1:12a uses the same wording, as far as possible, as in 1:10b (see also the various notes there).

The use of "the name of our Lord Jesus" rather than simply "our Lord Jesus" draws attention to that aspect of the character of the Lord Jesus which is particularly relevant in this context. That is to say, he himself will be praised, but the praise will focus on his character, presumably as Savior in this context where the praise arises either because of what he has done for his people, or from themselves directly—there being little difference. However, the difference between using "name" and not using it is rather subtle, so it is not represented (representing it as "character," say, would overemphasize it).

1:12b *And we pray this* **(1:11c–f) in order that you might be glorified by him,** The Greek representing this proposition is simply καὶ ὑμεῖς ἐν αὐτῷ 'and you in him', but the use of καί 'and' implies that the full clause (if written) would be "and in order that you may be glorified in him." In other words, it is the reciprocal equivalent of

1:12a, with "you" and "him" changing places. However, it is not presented as a precise reciprocal in the display for the following reasons:

1. It is much more common to speak of believers being glorified by or with Christ, rather than as being praised by him—hence, "glorified" is used as the translation of ἐνδοξάζω. (In 1:12a, "glorified" could be used, but it is semantically equivalent to "praised," so the simpler word is used.)
2. The prepositional phrase "in him" is so commonly used in the Pauline letters to mean "united to Christ" or "in union with him," that it has to be considered as a serious alternative here, even though there is, then, no close semantic parallel with the preceding ἐν phrase. Also, the parallel "because of what he has done for" does not work for this second phrase, as it would have to be completed to read "done for him," which makes no sense. Hence, although the two clauses are in a formal reciprocal relation, semantically, the reciprocal relation cannot be carried through strictly.

1:12c because God, whom we(inc) *worship/serve*, and our(inc) Lord Jesus Christ have acted graciously *toward you*. This proposition is based on a prepositional phrase introduced by κατά which commonly means "according to." However, especially when an event proposition is involved, κατά often introduces a reason for the preceding statements, and that is the case here.

The word used for "grace" here (χάρις) is the usual New Testament word, and is discussed in connection with 1:2a. Here it refers to God's freely bestowed and unmerited favorable actions towards sinful mankind, and so the display expression "act graciously" is used.

The expression τοῦ θεοῦ ἡμῶν 'the God of us' is used again, as in 1:11c, and is handled in the same way as there.

All the commentators discuss the question as to whether Jesus is actually called "God" here, i.e., whether the whole expression refers only to Jesus. This question arises because only one article is used and this generally means that only one person is referred to. Grammatically, therefore, it is indeed possible that it should be translated "our God and Lord, Jesus Christ," although even the KJV does not translate it like this (but see the NIV margin). However, the following arguments are urged against this exegesis:

1. The title "Lord" (κύριος), when used as a title, can readily occur without the article, so its absence from the second phrase may be quite normal.
2. Paul regularly associates God the Father and the Lord Jesus Christ as the source of grace in his greetings (as in 1:2), and there is no particular reason to understand this phrase as referring only to the Lord Jesus (both have already been referred to in this short paragraph).

Such an exegetical conclusion in no way reflects adversely on the doctrine of the full deity of Christ. In fact, so far as this verse is concerned, it is some liberal commentators who take it to refer to Jesus as God, and then conclude it is not a Pauline letter since Paul (or the church) did not hold such views of Christ at the time of Paul's ministry! The doctrine of Christ's deity is clear in every book in the New Testament, and is shown in many different ways, and does not in any way hinge on the exegesis of a single verse. The cumulative evidence is overwhelming.

BOUNDARIES AND COHERENCE

Verse 1:11 is marked as unit-initial by the occurrence of a new first person plural performative προσευχόμεθα 'we are praying'. Also, the initial clause is noticeably parallel with the initial clause in 1:3 (cf. "we ought to thank God always for you" and "we pray always for you"), and since it is also semantically distinct in content from the performative in 1:3, it is analyzed as the initiation of a new unit, not as the second part of the same unit.

Not only does 1:12 finish the Greek sentence begun in 1:11, but 2:1 is strongly marked with a change of genre to hortatory from expository.

Grammatically, these verses are formally tied together in a single sentence, the main (opening) clause being followed by a compound ἵνα '(in order) that' clause, and then a ὅπως '(further) in order that', and these formal signals indicate a unit tied together relationally in a close manner. There is no marked lexical coherence; "you" is overtly referred to in each of the three clauses, and so is "we." There are two semantic domains: one is that of God's activity ("consider worthy," "calling," "bring to completion, fulfill"—note also "grace" in the final phrase); and the other is that of the Thessalonian believers' character and activity ("desire," "goodness," "work," "faith").

PROMINENCE AND THEME

This is a typical orienter + content paragraph. The orienter is considered part of the theme since the paragraph is part of the introduction to the body of the letter, i.e., a "we-you" section. The content of the orienter is given in 1:11c–f. Proposition 1:11c is represented by the first ἵνα '(in order) that' clause, 1:11d–f by the second, the two being joined by καί 'and'. Semantically, however, they are not analyzed as of equal prominence, as on either analysis (see the notes), propositions 1:11d–f are considered to be supporting 1:11c, either as the means or as the specifics. Hence, the theme consists of 1:11b and c, omitting, however, the description proposition embedded in 1:11c and relating to God.

DIVISION CONSTITUENT 2:1–17 (Section: Nucleus₁ of the Body)

THEME: Continue believing the body of teaching which was committed to you by us(exc). In particular, do not be quickly troubled in mind and alarmed by any message that the Day of the Lord has already come.

RELATIONAL STRUCTURE	CONTENTS
SPECIFIC (negative)	2:1–12 Do not be quickly troubled in mind and alarmed by any message that the Day of the Lord has already come.
— grounds	2:13–14 God chose you and summoned you in order that you might be saved and glorified.
NUCLEUS	2:15 Continue believing the body of teaching which was committed to you by us(exc).
— means	2:16–17 We(exc) pray that our(inc) Lord Jesus Christ himself will encourage you and cause you to continue doing and speaking what is good.

BOUNDARIES AND COHERENCE

Verse 2:1 is marked as initial in a semantic unit by the occurrence of the particle δέ, a new performative ἐρωτῶμεν 'we request', and the occurrence of the vocative ἀδελφοί 'brothers'. Ἐρωτῶμεν is a hortatory performative, and it is the first such performative in the epistle. This occurrence, together with the fact that this is also the first δέ in the epistle, shows that Paul has moved from the introduction to the rest of the body, which, in this epistle, is basically hortatory material.

As already noted in connection with the discussion of the body, each of its constituent sections ends with a prayer. In the introduction to the body, (1:3–12) the prayer is introduced by a performative προσευχόμεθα 'we pray' (1:11), but in the rest of the body the prayers are marked by the use of δέ forefronting of the person prayed to, and the use of the optative mood. The first such prayer is found in 2:16–17, so 2:1–17 is analyzed as being the second body constituent. This final boundary is confirmed by the occurrence of τὸ λοιπόν 'finally' immediately following it in 3:1.

Coherence for this section is primarily relational, rather than referential, as various topics are dealt with in its main constituents. The first one (2:1–12, a paragraph cluster) centers on a negative command, not to be troubled in their minds by a false message that the day of the Lord had already come; the third constituent (2:15) is a generic positive command to hold firmly to what they had been taught by Paul and his associates. Hence, this unit centers on two commands, both dealing with teaching, true and false. In the second constituent (2:13–14), Paul encourages the Thessalonian believers by reminding them that they truly belong to God, for he has chosen them for himself and made them his own. And in the final constituent (2:16–17), Paul prays that the Lord would establish them as consistent, stable believers. Hence, this unit of 2:1–17 deals with the unsettledness, and even alarm, of the Thessalonians, arising from false teaching concerning the return of the Lord Jesus.

While I believe the above observations make a good case for 2:1–17 being a unit, it is not uncommon to find 2:1–12 and 2:13–17 treated as two comparable units, i.e., a major break is often considered to occur between 2:12 and 13. This is because 2:13 contains δέ, the vocative ἀδελφοί 'brothers', a performative "we ought to thank," and a change of topic. By way of comment on these observations, it should be noted that:

1. Each of the four main constituents posited in 2:1–17 begins with δέ or (in the case of 2:15) with ἄρα οὖν.
2. Each also begins with the vocative ἀδελφοί 'brothers', apart from the last (2:16–17), which is a prayer, making the use of ἀδελφοί 'brothers' obviously inappropriate.
3. Each has a change of topic.

In other words, the three criteria referred to above are analyzed as *paragraph* markers in Thessalonians, not *section* markers, a section having the further feature of a closing prayer, as well as an opening performative. However, the occurrence in 2:13 of the performative ὀφείλομεν εὐχαριστεῖν 'we ought to thank' (cf. 1:3) is certainly problematical. Two factors have led to the decision that it is not initiating a new unit, comparable to that initiated by 2:1:

1. The occurrence of the initial free pronoun ὑμεῖς 'we'.
2. The occurrence of a section-medial pair of performatives in 3:12.

Point 2 shows that performatives are not necessarily section-initial markers; and point 1 shows that, in fact, 2:13ff is closely tied to 2:1-12. The same phenomenon occurs in 3:13 (using ὑμεῖς 'you(pl)'), and again is closely tied to what precedes. In other words, there are good explanations available for the initial features of 1:13, and when these are weighed against the final prayers and the occurrence of τὸ λοιπόν 'finally', it is considered the best analysis to take chapter 2 as a single major constituent of the body, rather than two.

PROMINENCE AND THEME

Three factors lead to considering 2:15 as the nucleus unit in this section:

1. Relationally, the other units support it.
2. It occurs with the particle οὖν 'therefore', whereas all the other units only have δέ.
3. It is an affirmative command, and so ranks higher than the negative command of the first unit, the statement of the second unit, and the prayer of the last unit. (The prayer, like the command, would be a type of proposal, semantically, but a lower ranking one since the speaker ranks lower than the one addressed, unlike the command, where the reverse is the case.) Hence, 2:15, a propositional cluster in composition, is regarded as the most prominent unit in this section.

However, since the paragraph cluster 2:1-12 has a command for its theme, is much more developed than any of the other units, and is initial in the section, it is also considered to be prominent within the section. Hence, the theme consists of the positive generic command of 2:15 and the negative specific command which is the theme of 2:1-12. The specific is important because it is the particular problem to which the general command is applied in this epistle. To give only the generic command would leave out reference to about a quarter of the epistle, and, in effect, would leave out reference to one of the two issues that Paul deals with in this letter.

SECTION CONSTITUENT 2:1–12 (Paragraph Cluster: specific (neg.) of 2:15)

THEME: Do not be quickly troubled in mind and alarmed by any message that the Day of the Lord has already come.

RELATIONAL STRUCTURE	CONTENTS
EXHORTATION	2:1–3a Do not be quickly troubled in mind and alarmed by any message that the Day of the Lord has already come,
grounds — NUCLEUS	2:3b–5 since the Day of the Lord will come only after that time when the man who will sin very greatly will have been revealed by God.
circumstance₁	2:6–8 This man will be revealed by God when he who is now preventing him from being revealed will have been removed by God.
circumstance₂	2:9–12 When this man will be present, he will completely deceive those who will perish.

STRUCTURE OF 2:1–12

This semantic unit is analyzed as a *paragraph cluster*. A paragraph cluster is a group of paragraphs which functions as a unit parallel with simple paragraphs, i.e., as a constituent of a section rather than a division. Both of these conditions are fulfilled here. The display of these verses shows how the four paragraphs involved are related together in the way that propositional clusters and propositions are related within a paragraph, being closely linked formally; and the display of the role and prominence structure of the epistle shows that 2:1–12 is a constituent of section 2:1–17, along with 2:13–14, 2:15, and 2:16–17, the first and last of these being paragraphs, while 2:15 is a propositional cluster.

A similar, but alternative, analysis would be to see this cluster as consisting of a nucleus paragraph (2:1–3a) with a paragraph cluster functioning as its grounds. In this view, strictly speaking, 2:3b–12 would be a paragraph cluster, supporting a single paragraph. A paragraph supported by a paragraph cluster would tend to be analyzed as a section, which would then, along with the other paragraphs, be a constituent of the section 2:1–17.

It is the first of these two approaches that is preferred here, so the display and accompanying notes on 2:1–12 will be presented in four parts, corresponding to the four constituent paragraphs, viz., 2:1–3a, 3b–5, 6–8, 9–12.

BOUNDARIES AND COHERENCE

Since this is the first unit in the hortatory material of the body, it shares the opening boundary features of the vocative ἀδελφοί 'brothers', the hortatory performative ἐρωτῶμεν 'we are requesting', and the particle δέ.

After these initial features, a new topic is introduced by ὑπέρ 'concerning', the topic being "the coming of our Lord Jesus Christ and our being gathered to him."

The end of this unit is marked by the occurrence of a group of initial boundary features in 2:13 (for details, see Section Constituent 2:13–14).

This unit is built around several related topics: "the Day of the Lord" (which is inclusive of the coming of the Lord Jesus Christ and our being gathered to him); the "man of sin," also referred to as "the man of lawlessness" and "the lawless one"; and "those who will perish." These three topics cover all twelve verses as follows:

the Day of the Lord	2:1–3
the man of sin (etc.)	2: 3–10a
those who are perishing	2:10a–12

(See the display of this unit above.)

In connection with these three related topics, certain groups of lexical items are found:

1. Παρουσία 'presence, arrival' (2:1, 8, 9); ἀποκαλύπτω 'to reveal' (2:3, 6, 8); ἐπιφάνεια 'appearing' (2:8);

2. Ἁμαρτία 'sin' (2:3); ἀνομία 'lawlessness' (2:7); ἄνομος 'lawless' (2:8); ἀδικία 'wickedness' (2:10, 12);

3. Ἐξαπατάω 'deceive' (2:3); ἀπάτη 'deception' (2:10); ψεῦδος 'lie' (2:9, 11); πλάνη 'delusion, error'; and the contrasting item ἡ ἀλήθεια 'the truth' (2:10, 12); and

4. Ἀπώλεια 'destruction' (2:3); ἀπόλλυμι 'to destroy' (2:10); ἀναλίσκω/ἀναλόω/ἀναιρέω

'destroy' (2:8); καταργέω 'destroy, render utterly helpless'(2:8)

Grammatically, these verses are punctuated into six sentences: 2:1-4, 5, 6, 7, 8-10, 11-12. Significantly, all but one of the noninitial sentences begin with καί 'and' (2:6, 8, 11) or γάρ 'for' (2:7). The exception (2:5) is a rhetorical question and so has no formal link. These linking devices show that, though Paul is passing from one aspect to another, it is all within the same general topic. No δέ, showing a major shift of topic, is encountered until the new unit beginning at 1:13.

PROMINENCE AND THEME

This is a typical hortatory unit in which an initial exhortation (or exhortations) is supported by grounds for it. In this particular unit, the grounds are rather more elaborated, since Paul was refuting an error (cf. Col. 2:8-15 for a very similar example). The theme, then, is the initial exhortation. In this case, however, there are actually *two* commands, one in 1:2a, "Do not be quickly troubled in mind and alarmed," and the other in 1:3a, "do not be deceived by anyone in any way." Of these two, the former is chosen as the theme for the following reasons:

1. It occurs with the hortatory orienter "we are requesting you."
2. It includes the means by which the alarm and unsettledness was caused.
3. It stands in lexical contrast with the main exhortation of the primary matter, "stand firm."
4. The deception referred to in the second command can be regarded as the reason for the unsettledness and alarm, and the result ranks higher than the reason.

PARAGRAPH CLUSTER CONSTITUENT 2:1–3a (Paragraph: Nucleus of 2:1–12)

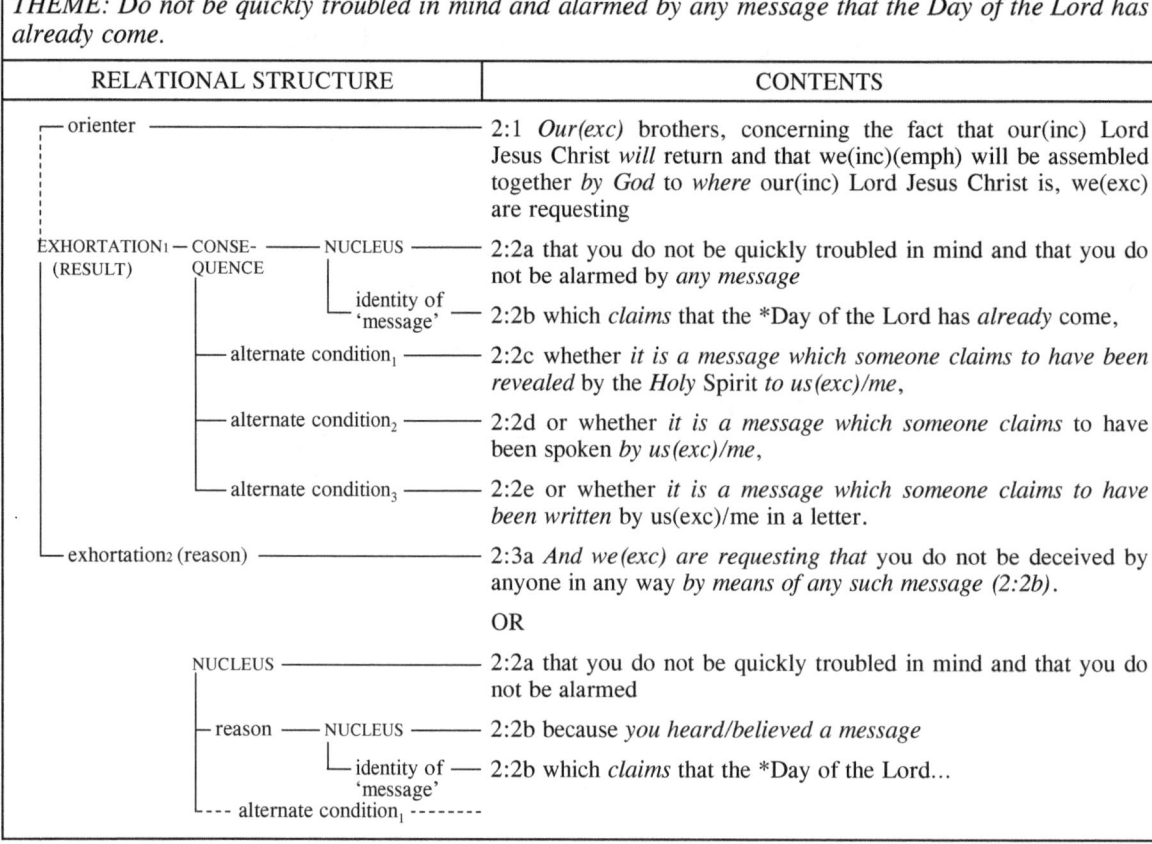

THEME: Do not be quickly troubled in mind and alarmed by any message that the Day of the Lord has already come.

NOTES

2:1 *Our(exc)* brothers, concerning the fact that our(inc) Lord Jesus Christ *will* return and that we(inc)(emph) will be assembled together *by God* to *where* our(inc) Lord Jesus Christ is, we(exc) are requesting The topic orienter introduces the subject of the next twelve verses, namely, the Lord's return. "The fact that" reflects the article in the Greek, which is interpreted to indicate that the topic, as such, was one already known to the Thessalonian Christians. (It was spelled out in 1 Thess. 4:13–17, as well as in Paul's oral teaching (see 2:5).) The active form "we(inc)(emph) will assemble together" is possible (the Greek has an abstract noun, ἐπισυναγωγῆς), but the passive is generally preferred (see 1 Thess. 4:17, where a passive verb is used). Some consider the noun to be a military term, equivalent to "muster."

The Greek word ἐρωτῶμεν, rendered "we(exc) are requesting" is appropriate between equals—Paul is not overtly asserting his apostolic authority here, but rather is cautioning them as a friend might do, as one concerned for their welfare.

2:2a that you do not be quickly troubled in mind and that you do not be alarmed by *any message* "Quickly" means since hearing this (false) message about the Day of the Lord. Some suggest the meaning "precipitately" or "hastily" or "soon after hearing."

The Greek underlying "troubled in mind" (σαλευθῆναι ... ἀπὸ τοῦ νοός 'be shaken from the mind') is hard to translate. Quite a variety of suggestions are given, but the idea seems to be that they no longer knew what to think about the Day of the Lord—had it come or had it not? This may be tied up with the second half of the topic orienter, in 2:1. Why did Paul mention this gathering together to Christ, which is not referred to again in this whole paragraph cluster? Quite possibly because it obviously had not happened, and hence, supported his rejection of this false teaching. But it could also be why the Thessalonians did not know what to think. If they believed, on the basis of Paul's teaching, that the Day of the Lord would see the Lord's return and their being gathered to him in the air, they might well be unsettled if someone said the Day of the Lord had arrived and yet they were still on earth in Thessalonica!

The Greek verb θροεῖσθαι 'be alarmed' is used elsewhere only in Matt. 24:6 and Mark 13:7, where it refers to alarm at "wars and rumors of wars." Morris (1959) suggests it means a state of "jumpiness" or "worry, being on edge, jittery"—a mixture of fear and worry.

It may be important for a translator to know whether the Thessalonians actually were, at the time of writing, upset, etc., or not. It seems most likely (cf. chap. 3) that a number were in this state, and the problem was spreading. Paul treats it as an actual problem, not a potential one.

2:2b–e which *claims* that the *Day of the Lord has *already* come, whether *it is a message which someone claims to have been revealed* by the *Holy* Spirit *to us(exc)/me*, or whether *it is a message which someone claims to have been spoken* by *us(exc)/me*, or whether *it is a message which someone claims to have been written* by us(exc)/me in a letter. The Greek underlying these propositions is very terse, literally, "whether by means of a spirit, or by means of a message, or by means of a letter as if by means of us, as that the Day of the Lord has arrived." The main question is: To how many of the preceding phrases is "as if by means of us" attached? There are three possible answers:

1. To the last only, to which it is immediately attached (cf. also 3:17).
2. To the last two, since they are again referred to in 2:15.
3. To all three, since they are symmetrically presented.

There seems little grounds on the basis of which to choose; the last is reflected in the display. In any case, it was obviously claimed that the message had Pauline authority. If the phrase is attached to the last only, or to the last two, then the first, "whether by means of a spirit (or (the) Spirit)," is generally taken as meaning a message immediately revealed to a prophet, a prophecy, probably in the Thessalonian congregation. (This would mean Paul was using "spirit" like John does in 1 John 4:1 and 3, as the supernatural source of a prophetic message.)

An alternative display is given for some of 2:2. In the main one, no implicit event is supplied in connection with "a message," and so no separate proposition is involved, as the relation is that of instrument within the proposition. In the alternate, the implicit events "to hear" or "to believe" are supplied, yielding a separate proposition. The relation is now that of reason; it was because they had heard this message that they were disturbed and alarmed. The relation of concession has been suggested—Paul was commanding them not to give way to the expected reactions of confusion and alarm. But Paul, himself, it seems reasonable to assume, did *not* expect them to be confused and alarmed—they should have known better. Hence, the relation of reason is preferred.

2:2b The expression "the Day of the Lord" has been retained in its literal form as a technical, eschatological term. If it is not possible to use a literal form in the translation (for example, because it now means "Sunday"), then it is probably best extended to the form "the day/time when the Lord will judge *all* people." (See, for example, the article "Day of the Lord" in Douglas 1977:296–7.) It is not a common expression in the New Testament; it is more common in the Old Testament, in the writings of the prophets. In the New Testament it is found in Acts 2:20 (in an Old Testament quote), 1 Cor. 1:8 ("the day of our Lord Jesus Christ"); 5:5 ("the day of (our) Lord (Jesus) (Christ)"—textual variants); 2 Cor. 1:14 ("the day of our Lord Jesus"); 1 Thess. 5:2; 2 Pet. 3:10 (= 1 Thess. 5:2); compare also the similar expressions in Phil. 1:6 ("day of Christ Jesus"); 1:10 and 2:16 ("day of Christ"). These references show that, in the New Testament, the Old Testament expression "Day of YHWH" was understood to refer to the "Day of the Lord Jesus Christ," he being God's appointed agent to carry out the events of that time. Hence, the textual variants of "Day of the Lord" and "Day of Christ" are not semantically significant, since it is the same "Day of the Lord Jesus Christ" that is being referred to.

It is more common in the New Testament to speak of the Lord's return (παρουσία) than of "the Day of the Lord"; see 2:1 and 8 in this epistle, and 1 Thess. 2:19, 3:13, 4:15, and 5:23. However, since both 1 Thess. 5:2 and 2 Pet. 3:10 state that "the Day of the Lord" will come "like a thief," this expression is generally regarded as referring to or including the παρουσία, or return, of the Lord, since he himself spoke of his return as being like a thief (in the night) (see Matt. 24:36-44, where παρουσία and "like a thief" are both used).

2:3a *And we(exc) are requesting that* you do not be deceived by anyone in any way *by means of any such message* (2:2b). This is a typical example of a third person imperative command in Greek, using the indefinite third person subject τις 'someone/anyone'. Semantically, third person commands are analyzed as second person commands addressed to the readers, and this approach is confirmed by the fact that the commands in 2:2a are direct, second person (plural) commands. So 2:3a is put in the form "We(exc) are requesting that you do not be deceived by anyone." The use of the aorist subjunctive may imply that the Thessalonians were in danger of being deceived, but were not actually deceived or perhaps a few of them were, but not the congregation as a whole.

What semantic relation is there between this command (prohibition) and those in 2:2? Clearly, it is not a matter of restatement (for emphasis) as the content is different. Rather, if, for the moment, the negative imperatives are disregarded, then there would seem to be a sequence of events, in which the false teaching was made known; it was believed to be true; by believing they were also being deceived since the teaching was, in fact, not true; believing it gave rise to alarm and unsettledness. In other words, Paul does not merely rebuke the unsettledness and alarm, but goes to the reason for it, and deals with that also. Since, however, the reason is given in the form of a command, it is considered to be prominent in this paragraph, but not equally prominent with the nucleus proposition (see earlier discussion). (If it is asked how a reason could be commanded, in this case, forbidden, the answer is that believing a message, and so being deceived by it, is a voluntary action and is therefore subject to a prohibition. It is analogous to commanded means.)

BOUNDARIES AND COHERENCE

The initial boundary has already been discussed under 2:1-12 and 2:1-17.

The paragraph is regarded as ending with 2:3a, which is a negative command. This is because 2:1 and 2 are clearly hortatory, and 2:3b introduces the grounds with a ὅτι 'because'. The command in 2:3a is clearly part of the exhortation, and not the grounds, so it is assigned to the nucleus paragraph. (Some have objected that it is very unnatural (if not unprecedented) to begin a paragraph with ὅτι 'because'. This is generally true, but in this case, since the grounds involves a considerable body of teaching, it is developed to consist of three short paragraphs. (Cf. also Col. 2:9 where expanded grounds are introduced by ὅτι.)

Relationally, this paragraph consists of two conjoined exhortations, prefaced by a topic orienter.

This paragraph is both tied together and demarked by the occurrence of references to "we" (four times in 2:1-2) and to "you(pl)" (four times in 2:1-3a), since there are no references to either of these in 1:3b-12.

PROMINENCE AND THEME

The two commands are the most prominent information in this paragraph. In discussing the theme of the whole paragraph cluster of 2:1-12, four arguments were presented for regarding the first of these two commands as the most prominent, and hence, thematic. The fourth of these arguments stated that the first command was a result, the second a reason, and the result is more prominent than the reason. For a discussion as to why the command in 2:3a is considered to be a reason for the command in 2:2a, see the notes on proposition 2:3a.

PARAGRAPH CLUSTER CONSTITUENT 2:3b–5
(Paragraph: Nucleus of 2:3b–12; grounds for 2:1–3a)

THEME: The Day of the Lord will come only after that time when the man who will sin very greatly will have been revealed by God.

RELATIONAL STRUCTURE	CONTENTS
NUCLEUS (topic)	2:3b *The Day of the Lord will come*
— conjoined	2:3c only after that time when *many people* will have rebelled *against God*
CONDITION — NUCLEUS — NUCLEUS	2:3d and only after that time when the man who will sin very greatly will have been revealed *by God*.
description₁ of 'the man'	2:3e This man will *certainly* be destroyed *by the Lord Jesus*;
description₂ of 'the man'	2:4a he will be the *supreme* enemy *of God*;
description₃ of 'the man' — REASON	2:4b and he will *proudly* exalt himself above everything that *people* consider *to be* God and above everything that *people* worship,
result	2:4c so that, *as a result* he will *even enter* God's temple and take his seat *there* and publicly proclaim that he himself is God.
orienter — NUCLEUS	2:5a I am sure that you remember that I kept telling you these things (2:3b–4c) [RHQ]
circumstance	2:5b while I was still with you *there in Thessalonica*.

NOTES

2:3b–c *The Day of the Lord will come* only after that time when *many people* will have rebelled *against God* There is no main clause expressed in the Greek, but it is clear from the context that it is in the form of 2:3b. Note, however, that there is, in effect, a double negation in the Greek: "the Day of the Lord will not come…if the rebellion does not come first." This has been expressed affirmatively in the display as "the Day of the Lord *will* come…only…." The ἐὰν μὴ…πρῶτον 'if not…first' in the double negation becomes "after" in the affirmative form.

Again, it is agreed that the article in ἡ ἀποστασία 'the rebellion' indicates two things, commonly signaled by the article in Greek. One is that the Thessalonians already knew about it (as 2:5 below confirms); and the other is that it is the supreme rebellion, the one which surpasses all others. (Some translations use "final" here.) The display use of "that time when" is an attempt to indicate these two uses of the article.

Ἀποστασία 'the rebellion' is an abstract noun, representing the event "to rebel." It is obvious from the following clauses that it is a rebellion against God. It is a rebellion in the sense of rejecting his authority, laws, ways, etc. It is not known whether it is Christians, Jews, or people in general who are involved (or all three), so the subject is kept vague with "many people."

2:3d and only after that time when the man who will sin very greatly will have been revealed *by God*. There is a textual choice between "man of sin" and "man of lawlessness." The UBS Textual Commentary (Metzger, 1971) says that the former is very well supported throughout the MSS, but the UBS text nonetheless has "lawlessness." The Majority Text has "sin." ("Lawlessness" is used below in 2:7, without variant.) In both cases, the force of the genitive construction is "(outstandingly) characterized by." "Lawlessness" has the idea, not so much of breaking the laws (of God), but rejecting them altogether, dispensing with them as irrelevant and undesirable. And the following verses (2:4–6) make it clear that his attitude to God's law is the expression of the same attitude to God himself. The Jerusalem Bible translates this expression with "the Rebel" and Giblin (1967) proposes "the Man of Rebellion."

The man referred to is said to be "revealed," and the same root is used as, was applied to the Lord Jesus in 1:7. Similarly, in 2:9, the term παρουσία 'coming' is used of this man, just as it is of Jesus in 2:1 and 8. There seems little doubt that parallels are being drawn between this man and the Lord Jesus, and consistency of terminology should be kept in the translation.

It is not certain how the καί 'and' linking the clauses which represent 2:3c and d is to be understood. It could either mean "and then" or "and, in particular." In any case, the two events are closely linked.

2:3e This man will *certainly* be destroyed *by the Lord Jesus*; This proposition is derived from another genitive construction "the son of the destruction," which again is very widely agreed to mean "one who is doomed to (final) destruction," someone who will certainly be destroyed. The implied agent is taken to be the Lord Jesus, because he is expressly said to destroy (though a different verb is used) the man of lawlessness in 2:8. An alternative exegesis is to take "son of destruction" as used in a parallel way to "sons of disobedience" (Eph. 2:2; 5:6; Col. 3:6) and "sons of light and sons of (the) day" (I Thess. 6:5), in which the noun in the genitive describes a predominant characteristic of the person referred to. This would give the sense "one who destroys (greatly)." This makes good sense in this list of bad characteristics of this man. It could be propositionalized in the form "This man will destroy *many things*." While this is contextually appropriate, and is parallel with Paul's use of the idiom "son(s) of..." elsewhere in his epistles, it is unlikely that the identical expression, used of Judas Iscariot in John 17:12, would have the active sense suggested here, "he who destroys." The more traditional passive sense "he who will be destroyed" is more likely to be the meaning in John.

2:4a-b he will be the *supreme* enemy *of God*; and he will *proudly* exalt himself above everything that *people* consider *to be* God and above everything that *people* worship, There is a choice of interpretation here. The Greek reads, ὁ ἀντικείμενος καὶ ὑπεραιρόμενος ἐπὶ πάντα λεγόμενον θεόν 'the one opposing and exalting over/against all called God...'. It would be possible to take both participles "opposing" and "exalting" as collocated with what follows to give "opposing all called God..." and "exalting over/against all called God." It is objected to this that the preposition ἐπί, which can be translated either "over" or "against," while appropriate for the second participle, is collocationally inappropriate for the first. (In the New Testament, ἀντίκειμαι 'to oppose' takes the dative case for what is opposed.) Consequently, most commentators, and some versions, take the first as a separate phrase, meaning "the opponent" or "the enemy," i.e., the supreme, unique, outstanding one. If taken this way, he is utterly opposed to God. If the other interpretation is preferred, care should be taken, as the UBS Handbook indicates, to avoid giving the impression that this man's opposition to anything that people worship (such as idols, fetishes, ancestors, etc.) is a *virtue*; rather, it means this man utterly repudiates all that is worshiped in favor of *himself* being worshiped, as comes out clearly at the end of 2:4.

2:4c so that, *as a result,* he will *even enter* God's temple and take his seat *there* and publicly proclaim that he himself is God. The Greek for the first part of 2:4c is εἰς τὸν ναὸν τοῦ θεοῦ καθίσαι 'into the temple of God to sit down', so an implicit event "to enter" has been supplied in 2:4c, implied by the use of εἰς 'into'.

There is no agreement as to whether "God's temple" (or "shrine," ναός) refers to the temple at Jerusalem, or the Christian Church, or possibly some other place. Since this is unfulfilled prophecy, the translator is encouraged to preserve the ambiguous reference if at all possible.

"Take his seat" is intended to reflect an official act, not just sitting down. As the commentators point out, even Antiochus Epiphanes and Caligula only put images in the temple at Jerusalem; this man puts himself there. However, it is quite possible that "to take his seat" is a metonymy for what a person does who occupies an official seat. For examples of this in the New Testament, see Matt. 19:28 and 1 Cor. 6:4, "function as a judge"; Matt. 23:2 "be an official interpreter (of Moses' writings)"; Matt. 20:23, Eph. 1:20, Rev. 3:21 "rule over others (like a king)." If καθίζω 'to take one's seat' is figurative, then it is much more likely that ναός 'temple/shrine' refers to the Church, and this man is portrayed as the supreme false prophet, trying to tell the Church what it should believe and do, i.e., usurping Christ's place, who is "seated" (καθίζω) at God's right hand.

2:5a–b I am sure that you remember that I kept telling you these things (2:3b–4c) [RHQ] while I was still with you *there in Thessalonica*. This is a rhetorical question. Its form in the Greek (with an initial οὐ) implies that Paul expected that they did remember. So the display uses "I am sure that you remember."

It is very widely agreed that "these things" (ταῦτα) refers back to what Paul has just been saying in 2:3–4. Ταῦτα can also refer forward, but if that is so, it seems awkward to follow it immediately with "you know," rather than a direct statement of what they remembered. Also, the use of καί 'and' at the beginning of 2:6 indicates the start of another aspect of this teaching.

The imperfect tense of the verb λέγω 'to tell' almost certainly implies that Paul had taught them about the rebellion, the man of sin, etc., on a number of occasions while in Thessalonica. "I told you a number of times" would be an alternative representation.

This rhetorical question closes off one aspect of Paul's topic, namely, the character and activities of the man of sin, who precedes the Day of the Lord; in 2:6, Paul turns to a different aspect. Hence, 2:5 is analyzed as a closing orienter.

BOUNDARIES AND COHERENCE

This paragraph (and its supporting paragraphs) are introduced by ὅτι and constitute the (prophetic) grounds for the warnings in 2:1–3a.

It ends with the rhetorical question of 2:5. (For a discussion of whether this rhetorical question terminates or initiates a unit, see the notes on 2:5a–b.)

The general topic of paragraph cluster 2:1–12 is the Lord's return (= the Day of the Lord); 2:3 introduces the particular topic of the grounds (2:3b–12) which is the "man of sin" or the "man of lawlessness." More strictly speaking, the topic is "the revealing of the man of sin," referred to, as topic, in 2:3, 8, and 9, i.e., once in each of the grounds paragraphs.

There is also a switch from a hortatory paragraph (2:1–3a) to an expository one.

This paragraph is closely bound together by a string of references to the man of sin/lawlessness:

the man of sin/lawlessness	2:3
the son of destruction	2:3
the opponent/enemy	2:4
the one who exalts himself	2:4
the one who takes his seat in God's temple	2:4
the one who declares that he is God	2:4

PROMINENCE AND THEME

As already noted, this is an unusual paragraph in that the formal grammatical nucleus is implicit. But it is very readily supplied from the flow of the argument, and would be "the day of the Lord will not come." This is then immediately followed by two conjoined clauses, introduced by ἐὰν μή 'unless'. It is clear, however, that the nucleus proposition cannot state that "the day of the Lord will not come." The negative of the implicit nucleus clause, together with the negative of the "unless" clauses, is semantically equivalent to "the day of the Lord will come only if...." Of the two conjoined conditions, it is the second, with its reference to the revealing of the man of sin/lawlessness, which is considered the more prominent of the two. This is because it introduces the topic of the grounds, that is developed, in various ways, in the following paragraphs. Since the main "unless" clause is an event, and a future event, the form of the theme becomes "only after..." rather than "only if." It is worth noting, in connection with the theme, that it is implied by Paul's whole argument here that the man of sin/lawlessness had not yet been revealed at the time he was writing.

PARAGRAPH CLUSTER CONSTITUENT 2:6–8
(Paragraph: circumstance₁ of 2:3b–5)

THEME: This man will be revealed by God when he who is now preventing him from being revealed will have been removed by God.

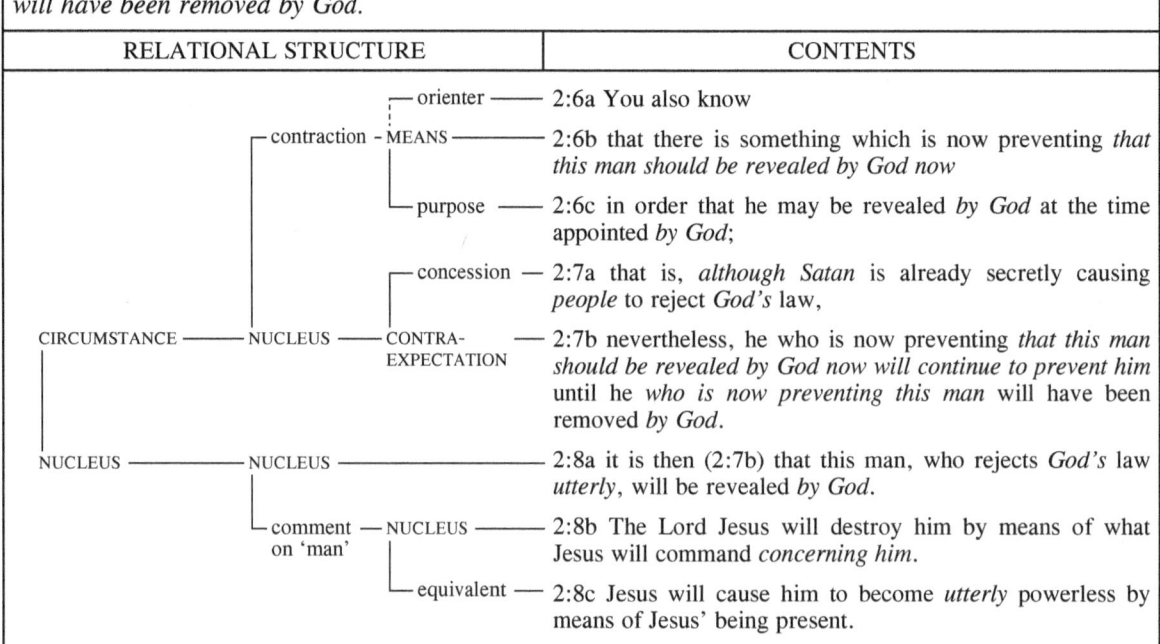

NOTES

2:6a–b You also know that there is something which is now preventing *that this man should be revealed by God now* The Greek clause which represents these propositions has just five words καί νῦν το κατέχον οἴδατε 'and now that-which is-preventing you-know', but they have provoked a great deal of discussion.

An important question is: What part of the clause is νῦν 'now' connected with? Three possibilities are suggested:

1. It goes with καί 'and' so functions as a conjunction with the sense of "therefore" (i.e., a conclusion from preceding statements) or "next" (indicating a transition to a new topic, or aspect of one). However, Arndt and Gingrich give only temporal meanings for νῦν, and this conclusion is supported by independent research by John Werner and myself. Hence, it is not considered to have the sense of "therefore" or "next."

2. It goes with οἴδατε 'you know. While this is possible, it would be semantically redundant. If they know, then they know now, and it is hard to avoid the impression that if the νῦν is connected with "you know," then there is an implied contrast with a time when they did not know, especially since νῦν is the first word after the conjunction. But there is no such contrast, and the use of καί, rather than δέ, strengthens this view. (Paul, when using "now" contrastively with what precedes, regularly uses νυνὶ δέ.)

3. It goes with τὸ κατέχον 'that which is preventing'. This construction consists of an article and a present participle and it is argued by some of the older commentators that if νῦν were connected with τὸ κατέχον, then it would be placed between the article and the participle, to give τὸ νῦν κατέχον. It is quite true that this syntactic pattern is found a number of times in the New Testament, particularly in Paul's letters (e.g. Rom. 3:26; 8:18; 1 Tim. 6:17; Tit. 2:12) and Peter also speaks of οἱ νῦν οὐρανοί 'the present heavens', i.e., the ones in existence now. Only one of Paul's uses involves a participle, but that is very similar: (τοῦ πνεύματος) τοῦ νῦν ἐνεργοῦντος '(the spirit) the one now working' i.e., the spirit who is currently at work (Eph. 2:2).

Argument 3 would seem to be basically sound, but there is a good reason for this normal pattern not being followed here, namely, that this clause is in contrast with the following one in two respects:

1. "Being prevented" is in contrast with "being revealed."
2. "Now" is in contrast with the future reference of "in his own (proper) time."

Hence, the νῦν is brought forward because of the contrast, the clauses being in a sort of chiastic pattern:

A now
  B preventing
  B' revealed
A' in his own time

The two times are at the outside edge of the chiasmus, and probably, therefore, prominent.

The conclusion, then, is that νῦν goes with τὸ κατέχον 'that which is preventing', has the meaning "now, at the present time," and is in contrast with ἐν τῷ ἑαυτοῦ καιρῷ 'in his own time' in the following clause. It is worth adding that the fact that τὸ κατέχον 'that which is preventing' precedes the verb indicates that it is the new paragraph topic, which runs through 2:6-8.

The use of καί 'and' (rather than δέ), the use of οἴδατε 'you know', and the use of the article in τὸ κατέχον, all point to the fact that Paul is simply reminding the Thessalonians of what they already know. This is not new teaching for them. However, as a glance at the commentaries will quickly show, we do not know what Paul was referring to, and there are many different views as to what it is that is "preventing" (see the following note).

The verb κατέχω, from which the participle κατέχον comes, is a transitive verb, so the question arises: What was being prevented (or restrained, or held back)? The answer is provided by the main topic of 2:3d-12, namely "the revealing of the man of sin." It is his being revealed that is being prevented by some unidentified power, force, principle, etc., (the Greek is neuter). This analysis is confirmed by the following clause, which explains why his appearance is being prevented—it is in order that he may appear only at his appointed time—not before he is due, not after, but just at the right moment.

Questions are raised in the commentaries, etc., as to just what the verb κατέχω does mean here. Its fifteen New Testament occurrences are confined to Luke's writings, Paul's letters, and Hebrews. Three classes of collocates can be distinguished (ignoring the special collocates in Luke 14:19, "the lowest seat..." and Acts 27:40 (nautical)): things, persons, and messages or qualities of character. With things, it means "to possess" (1 Cor. 7:30; 2 Cor. 6:10); with persons, "to keep a person in a place, prevent them from going somewhere or doing something" (Luke 4:42; Phlm. 13; and presumably Rom. 7:6); with a message, or Christian qualities of character, it means "hold on to, retain, keep on believing or practicing" (Luke 8:15; 1 Cor. 11:2; 15:2; 1 Thess. 5:21; Heb. 3:6, 14; 10:23).

It has been argued above that the implicit object of τὸ κατέχον is αὐτόν 'him', i.e., the man of sin, so here the sense of κατέχω with a person is required, and the generally accepted sense of "to restrain, prevent, hold back" fits very well with this study of the collocates of κατέχω.

2:6c in order that he may be revealed *by God* at the time appointed *by God*; Quite a lot has been said about this proposition already in the preceding notes; one further comment is needed.

The verb form ἀποκαλυφθῆναι 'to be revealed', is passive so the question arises as to the agent. This question is best answered by considering the time phrase ἐν τῷ ἑαυτοῦ καιρῷ 'in the season of himself'. This does not mean "when he chooses" as is clear from Paul's further explanation in 2:7-8, but rather (as most of the commentators point out) at the time God has determined for his appearance. Hence, the agent is considered to be God, and the sense of ἑαυτοῦ 'of himself' is "at his own proper (time)," i.e., "at the time when he ought to appear," which, in the context, is a time determined by God.

The word translated "time" is καιρός, which commonly has the sense of "a particular time," "a time that is significant" in some way.

2:7a that is, *although Satan* is already secretly causing *people* to reject *God's* law, This is a very difficult clause to express in propositional form. What it says literally is "for the mystery of lawlessness is already at work" (τὸ γὰρ μυστήριον ἤδη ἐνεργεῖται τῆς ἀνομίας.)

The word translated "lawlessness" is ἀνομίας, a noun corresponding to the adjective ἄνομος 'lawless' used at the beginning of the next verse. And it is the same as the possible reading in 2:3, 'the man of lawlessness'. It has the same sense in each of these places of open defiance and rejection of, or opposition to, God's law, this being considered as an expression of God's will for man's life. In line with his claim to be God (2:4), this man utterly repudiates God's revealed will (quite possibly substituting his own).

But what is τὸ μυστήριον...τῆς ἀνομίας 'the mystery...of lawlessness'? "Mystery" is generally considered to have the same sense here as elsewhere in Paul's writings, i.e., a truth which man cannot discover by himself, but which God has made known. What Paul appears to be saying is that the principle of opposition to God's law (or revealed truth) is already at work—such opposition is already present, but, because of some restraining force also at work, this principle is only covertly at work. In fact, it will only come into the open, and be clearly revealed, when the man of lawlessness himself appears (cf. 2:8a). Verse 2:9, with its reference to Satan working powerfully, may well imply that this working of lawlessness is essentially a Satanic activity, covert at the present time, but to be revealed at the right moment (2:8a). Hence, proposition 2:7a can be stated in the form: "that is, although *Satan* is already secretly causing *people* to reject *God's* law."

The verb used here, ἐνεργέω (in the middle voice), is cognate with the noun ἐνέργεια used in 2:9 and 11 below, and carries the implication of effective work, work that produces results.

The γάρ 'for' is considered to introduce an explanatory expansion of 2:6b-c. This expansion makes clear that lawlessness is already at work, and that if there were no restraining power, it might well produce the man of sin before his appointed time. But it also goes on to make clear that the time will come when this restraining power/person is removed, i.e., ceases to act in this way (see 2:7b below).

2:7b nevertheless, he who is now preventing *that this man should be revealed by God now will continue to prevent him* until he *who is now preventing this man* will have been removed *by God*. This propositional cluster corresponds to only one clause in the original Greek, μόνον ὁ κατέχων ἄρτι ἕως ἐκ μέσου γένηται 'only he who prevents now until out of the middle he becomes'.

Ὁ κατέχων ἄρτι 'he who prevents now' clearly corresponds to νῦν τὸ κατέχον 'that which is preventing now' in 2:6a, even though there is a switch from the neuter "that which" to the masculine "he who," and from νῦν now, to ἄρτι 'now'. The former switch would appear to imply that whatever it is that is restraining the man of sin is not a purely impersonal force; there is a person behind that force. Paul tells us no more; so again, there are many different opinions as to who "he" might be. The switch from νῦν to ἄρτι may be purely for stylistic variation, or possibly because they are involved in different contrasts; there is no difference in meaning in this context.

Ἕως ἐκ μέσου γένηται 'until out of the middle he becomes' defines the end of the period during which "the mystery of lawlessness" is at work, or since there is a restraint in operation, the period during which this evil activity has to be covert, an "independent" operation. "Out of the middle he becomes" is generally regarded as meaning "to be removed" (as a hindrance is removed). It says nothing of how this is effected, whether it is sudden or gradual, by force or by other means. However, it is argued by Barnouin (1977) that ἐκ μέσου γίνομαι does not mean "is removed." He maintains that this particular collocation is not found in Greek literature, apart from the writings of Plutarch, and there it refers to leaving a particular group of people, such as a political group. Hence, Barnouin suggests the translation here "until he comes out of the state of restriction" (already referred to earlier in the verse). However, Barnouin considers that the "man of sin" is the (implicit) subject of ἐκ μέσου γένηται. The analysis presented here follows the more commonly preferred view that it is "the preventer" who is the subject. This would then give ἐκ μέσου γένηται the sense of "leave off performing something," "relinquish a particular activity." In the display this would give "until he...ceases doing this." The only real difference between these two views is that the former is passive, the latter active. In the overall context, the passive is preferable, with God the implicit agent.

But what does μόνον 'only' mean here? Giblin (1967:210-214) discusses the meaning of clause-initial μόνον in 1 Cor. 7:39, Gal. 2:10, 5:13, 6:12, and Phil. 1:27. His conclusion is that it expresses a "restrictive conditional force." In terms of the relations used in SSAs, this corresponds to certain types of concession-contraexpectation, i.e., μόνον signals the contraexpectation. Hence, 2:7a is analyzed as a concession, 2:7b as the corresponding contraexpectation.

2:8a it is then (2:7b) that this man, who rejects *God's* law *utterly*, will be revealed *by God*. This is the third reference to the man of sin, or the lawless man, each coupled with the verb ἀποκαλύπτω (passive) 'to be revealed'. The others are in 2:3 and 6.

The τότε 'then' is generally considered to be emphatic, i.e., "it is at that very time that," and it clearly refers back to the removal of the restrainer; "...it indicates the point of special interest with reference to the topic treated in the immediate context" (Giblin 1967:232, fn. 1).

2:8b The Lord Jesus will destroy him by means of what Jesus will command *concerning him*. The events referred to in 2:8b and c take place at the time of the Lord's return as is made clear by the use of παρουσία (see also 2:1) at the end of 2:8. In other words, in 2:6–8 there is a time sequence of (a) the man of sin being restrained, (b) the restraint being removed, (c) the man of sin being revealed, (d) the return of the Lord Jesus, and (e) the destruction of the man of sin. There is some doubt as to whether "Jesus" is in the original text, or not, but there is good evidence for its presence, and, in any case, many translations will need to identify "Lord" more specifically with the name Jesus. In addition to this question of the text, there are two matters here:

1. There is first another question concerning the text—is the verb ἀνελεῖ or ἀναλώσει? In this context, however, they have virtually the same sense of "get rid of by killing or executing," so the translator is unaffected.
2. In the original, and in almost all versions, it has "by means of the breath (or spirit) of his mouth." What does this mean? Interestingly enough, almost all the commentators insist upon it being taken literally, as if Jesus were to blow upon the man of sin. This seems most unlikely to be the meaning, and, in fact, would not really tie in well with the repeat statement in the following clause. Assuming, therefore, that it is figurative, there seem to be two possibilities of understanding what it refers to:
   a. The ease, one might say, the effortless ease, with which the Lord Jesus will deal with the man of sin. One puff, so to speak, and he is gone!
   b. The "breath of his mouth" is a figurative way of referring to what the Lord Jesus says (or commands) with respect to the man of sin. Just as the world was created at his command and as people were healed, so will this man be executed by the command of the Savior; one word is enough!

Since the idea expressed in b is well supported elsewhere in scripture (though not the expression itself), it *is* given preference over alternative a, which is not attested as an idiom for "easily" elsewhere.

2:8c Jesus will cause him to become *utterly powerless by means of Jesus' being present*. A different, but parallel, verb, καταργέω, 'abolish' is used in this second statement. With beings as object, it has the sense of "rob of their power, render powerless, reduce to a powerless state." In the light of the previous proposition, this is evidently achieved by killing the man.

Parallel to the earlier expression τῷ πνεύματι τοῦ στόματος αὐτοῦ 'by means of the breath of his mouth' there is the expression τῇ ἐπιφανείᾳ τῆς παρουσίας αὐτοῦ 'by means of the manifestation of his coming'. The word translated by "manifestation" is ἐπιφάνεια, also translated "appearing." It tends to be used in Greek of the appearance of deity, and the emphasis here is on the fact that the Lord Jesus has only to appear for the man of sin to be overthrown. His presence is sufficient. (Whether there is also a component of "suddenly," or "unexpectedly," in the use of ἐπιφάνεια here is uncertain.)

It is not at all easy to decide how the propositional cluster of 2:8b–c is related to what precedes. Various factors need to be borne in mind:

1. The topic throughout these verses is the revealing of the man of sin, and not only is this referred to quite explicitly in 2:8a, but is taken up again in 2:9–10.
2. Although a time sequence can be seen in 2:6–8, Paul is not presenting a time-scheme, but rather discussing the fact that the man of sin will be revealed before the Lord returns.
3. The clauses represented by 2:8b–c are introduced by the relative pronoun ὅν 'whom' (i.e., the lawless man). In Greek, this construction can either introduce background information, or signal a switch to a new aspect of a major topic or a new topic. Since Paul continues with his main topic in 2:9, it seems reasonable to conclude that this is background or subordinated information. Since it does not describe or identify the man of sin, as such, but rather

spells out his fate, it is labeled "comment" on the man of sin, and this would tie in with the fact that the relation of comment and backgrounded information seem commonly to go together.

BOUNDARIES AND COHERENCE

This paragraph starts after the rhetorical question in 2:5, and this is confirmed by the topicalization (by forefronting) of τὸ κατέχον 'that which prevents'.

It is more difficult to decide where this paragraph ends. The arguments are the following:

1. The topic of "that which (or he who) prevents" the lawless man from appearing continues clearly through 2:6 and 7, and it is not referred to thereafter. Hence, it could be argued that paragraph ends with 2:7 and the next one starts with 2:8.
2. The opening words of 2:8 are καὶ τότε ἀποκαλυφθήσεται ὁ ἄνομος 'and then shall be revealed the lawless one. This is a restatement of the overall grounds topic. Further, it is repeated at the beginning of 2:9, in broadly synonymous terms οὗ ἐστιν ἡ παρουσία 'whose presence (coming) is...'. It is argued therefore that preference should be given to an analysis in which the grounds topic is restated explicitly in each paragraph, rather than having it implied, but not stated, in one of them (i.e., 2:6-7). Hence, it is proposed that 2:8a (at least) should be grouped with 2:6-7, to give an explicit statement of the grounds topic in 2:6-8a.
3. As stated in argument 2, the opening statement of 2:8 is strongly implied by 2:6-7, and so would have to be supplied in any propositional rewrite. In addition, the τότε 'then' of 2:8a refers back to 2:6-7, so the content of 2:6-7 is referred to in 2:8 anaphorically.
4. The real problem is that after these opening words in 2:8, Paul goes on to describe the overthrow of the lawless one, before returning in 2:9 to the main topic of the lawless one's activities before he is overthrown. So a plausible analysis would be to make 2:6-8a one distinct unit, 2:8b another, and 2:9-12 a third. The main arguments against taking 2:8b as a separate unit are:
   a. It is sandwiched between two statements of the main topic, and so gives the impression of diverging from it.
   b. It is a "flash-forward" to a time beyond that of the paragraph that follows (2:9-12). While Paul does not wish the Thessalonians to be in any doubt as to the fate of this supremely evil man, it is not part of his main topic, which is the activities of this man.

Hence, it is concluded that 2:6-8 forms a semantic unit in which the nonappearance of the lawless man at the time of Paul's writing is explained.

PROMINENCE AND THEME

The prominence structure of this paragraph is not at all straightforward. The paragraph topic τὸ κατέχων 'that which prevents' is announced in the first independent clause, it being understood from the topic of 2:3b-12 that what is being prevented is the man of sin from being revealed. What Paul then makes clear is that a time, determined by God, will come when whatever it is that prevents the man of sin's appearance will be removed. It is then that the man will be able to appear, and will, in fact, do so.

The other independent clause is 2:8a, καὶ τότε ἀποκαλυφθήσεται ὁ ἄνομος 'and it is then that the lawless man will be revealed'. The main topic is "the lawless man will be revealed," so clearly the information contributed by 2:6-7 is intended to explain more precisely when "then" is. This is defined by the clause immediately preceding 2:8a, which states that whoever is preventing this man from appearing will be removed. Hence, the topic of this paragraph is "something/someone is preventing that the man of sin be revealed," and the comment on this topic is that the time will come when whatever/whoever is doing this preventing will be removed by God.

PARAGRAPH CLUSTER CONSTITUENT 2:9-12
(Paragraph: circumstance₂ of 2:3b-5)

THEME: When this man will be present, he will completely deceive those who will perish.

RELATIONAL STRUCTURE	CONTENTS
CIRCUMSTANCE	2:9a **When** this man will be present,
— nucleus₁	2:9b he *will be* empowered by Satan with very great power,
— nucleus₂	2:9c and he *will do supernatural* signs and amazing deeds, which will seem like *God caused them to be done*,
NUCLEUS₃ RESULT	2:10a and he will completely deceive by wicked *deeds* those who will *certainly* perish.
— reason — REASON	2:10b *He will deceive them* because they will have refused to love the true *message*;
— result	2:10c as a result, they will not be saved *by God*.
— reason — RESULT MEANS — REASON	2:11a Because *they did* this (2:10b), God will cause by his power that they *who will perish* will be gullible
— result	2:11b so that, *as a result*, they will believe that which *this man* falsely claims
— purpose	2:12 in order that everyone who did not believe the true *message* but who gladly chose *to be doing* what is wicked will be *justly* condemned *by God*.

NOTES

2:9a When this man will be present, With this proposition, Paul returns to the topic of 2:3b-12, that is, the events associated with the appearance of the man of sin. This return is signaled in the Greek by a relative clause whose subject is a nominalized reference to the man of sin's appearance. In this case, however, Paul uses the word παρουσία 'presence' that he has just used of Christ's second coming, once again making a parallel between the man of sin and Christ. However, Christ is returning, the man of sin is not; so the word is used in its primary sense of "be present" (without implication as to how the person came to be present). If the lexical link can be maintained in a translation, that is preferable.

The topic, since it is a proposition relating to a future event, takes the form of a "when" clause in the display, but some other form might be appropriate in another language.

2:9b he *will be* empowered by Satan with very great [HYP] power, The Greek word translated by "*will be* empowered" is an abstract noun ἐνέργειαν 'operation', which Arndt and Gingrich point out is used only with "supernatural beings." It is used again in 2:11a, where it is translated by "will cause by...power."

The first of the three nouns used here (δυνάμει 'power') is singular, the other two being plural; "all" (πάσῃ) is also singular. Since δύναμις 'power' is used in the plural along with the following words in other contexts (e.g. Acts 2:22), the singular here is regarded as significant. Satan's empowering will be characterized by very great power, πάσῃ 'all' being regarded as hyperbolic here, and this great power will show itself in false signs and miracles.

2:9c and he *will do supernatural* signs and amazing deeds, which will seem like *God caused them to be done*, The force of the Greek is that the man of sin's presence will be marked by, or accompanied by, miracles; but it seems generally agreed that he himself will do them (although the possibility of close associates also doing so is not precluded by the Greek). Again, a parallel with the Lord's ministry is obviously being made (cf. Acts 2:22). The terms used are probably meant to be comprehensive for all types of miraculous deeds.

Most versions describe these deeds as "false," which in this context means "apparently done by God's power, but not actually so." The Greek word translated "false" (ψεῦδος) is used again in 2:11, where it is usually translated "the lie" (see 2:11b).

2:10a and he will completely deceive by wicked *deeds* those who will *certainly* perish. There is a genitive construction underlying this proposition, viz., πάσῃ ἀπάτῃ ἀδικίας 'all deceit of wickedness/unrighteousness'. Various suggestions are made for the meaning signaled by this genitive construction. The two most likely in this context are that the deceit springs from wickedness, i.e., wicked motives, or that it is brought about by various wicked means. While the former is undoubtedly true, the latter seems preferable, as this is best regarded as a summary statement of what just precedes, i.e., the various miraculous deeds, but it also includes any other wicked means used. The πάσῃ 'all', when related to the event concept "to deceive" (ἀπάτη 'deceit'), has the sense of "utterly" or "completely."

While the Greek is literally "the ones perishing" (τοῖς ἀπολλυμένοις), the reference is future (since the whole context is future), and it is very widely agreed that there is the implicit idea that their fate is certain, which is supported by the statements in the rest of this same verse.

2:10b *He will deceive them* because they will have refused to love the true *message*; While this proposition is clearly marked as a reason in the Greek by the use of the conjunction ἀνθ' ὧν (rather rare; used elsewhere only in Luke 1:20; 12:3; 19:44; and Acts 12:23), there are two possibilities for the result of which it is the reason. One is the whole proposition 2:10a, i.e., they are deceived completely because...; the other is just the final identification proposition, i.e., they will perish because.... The second view appears to be the common one, but the former fits in better with the overall thrust of 2:9-12, which develops, at some length, the idea that the man of sin will deceive people, why this is, the consequences of it, etc. On either view, Paul takes up a new (minor) topic here, "those who will perish," and develops it.

The Greek collocations in this clause are unique, τὴν ἀγάπην τῆς ἀληθείας οὐκ ἐδέξαντο 'they did not accept/welcome the love of the truth'. This is obviously roughly equivalent to "they did not believe the truth" (2:12a), but the unusual form of expression is generally considered to intensify the simple statement in the direction of "they deliberately and gladly rejected the truth." And what they gladly embraced instead is also given in 2:12a: "they gladly chose what is wicked."

Ἀλήθεια 'the truth' refers to the whole of the gospel message, God's revelation to men. It is in clear antithesis in this passage to "the lie" of the man of sin (2:9, 11).

2:10c as a result, they will not be saved *by God*. This proposition corresponds to εἰς τὸ σωθῆναι αὐτούς 'to the end that they be saved.' The Greek here is elliptical, as it says, literally, "they did not welcome the love of the truth in order to be saved." One has to welcome the truth to be saved. What is missing is "If they had welcomed the truth [in order to be saved], they would have been saved; [but they did not]." The simplest way to handle this in the display is to put the negative back into proposition 2:10c, and treat it as a result, i.e., they refused the truth, and so were not saved.

2:11a Because *they did* this (2:10b), God will cause by his power that they *who will perish* will be gullible The Greek corresponding to the first part of this constituent is simply καὶ διὰ τοῦτο 'and because of this'. The τοῦτο 'this' refers back to the statement that they rejected the truth. The following statement that God causes them to be deluded into accepting the man of sin's claims is seen as God's judicial blinding of those who refuse to see (cf. the similar cases of Pharaoh's hardening of his heart, and the homosexuals of Rom. 1). The UBS Handbook, however, sees this phrase as meaning "this is because," and hence, introducing a reason for what is stated previously for it. However, no other such examples of διὰ τοῦτο functioning in this way are cited, and such an analysis would also imply that the reason they refused to love the truth was that God caused them to be deluded. However, since refusing to love the truth refers to their rejection of the gospel, this makes God responsible for that rejection without any obvious reason for such an action on his part. Their rejection, a deliberate and willing rejection, however, followed by God's judicial action in response to that rejection, is a normal scriptural pattern of events.

However, the relationships are still somewhat complex, as two results are given as arising from one reason. The reason is their rejection of the truth: the first result stated is their being deceived by the man of sin (2:10a); the second result stated is that God causes them to be deluded (2:11a). However, this being deluded is followed by the result (or purpose) of that delusion, namely, believing the man of sin's claims (2:11b). Hence, the temporal order of events is:

1. They refused the truth (2:10b);
2. God caused them to be deluded (2:11a); and
3. They believed the man of sin's claims (2:10a, 11b).

But, for thematic reasons, these events are presented in the order 3–1–2–3', event 3 being given in two separate forms, first and last. Thematically, however, 3 is the paragraph nucleus, and 1 directly supports it. Further, 3' clearly supports 2; so the problem is: What is the prominence relation between 1 and 2? Event 2 is considered not to outrank 1, because if it did, it would be of the same rank as the nucleus statements, but since 2 does not deal directly with the man of sin's coming, this is considered erroneous. Event 2 could support 1, but this is considered implausible because 2 is in a semi-independent form, with an indicative verb and no subordinating conjunction, only καὶ διὰ τοῦτο 'and because of this'. So 2 and 1 are considered to be of equal rank semantically.

The Greek corresponding to the second part of this constituent is πέμπει αὐτοῖς ὁ θεὸς ἐνέργειαν πλάνης 'God sends to them a working of delusion'. Semantically, this is equivalent to the future statement "God will cause, by his power, that they will be deluded." In other words, the genitive construction ἐνέργειαν πλάνης 'a working of delusion' is understood to mean "a working that results in delusion." Although "delusion" is the common English translation of πλάνης here, the display has used "gullible," because God's judgment takes the form of their being ready to believe anything, since they will not believe the truth.

2:11b so that, *as a result,* they will believe that which *this man* falsely claims The Greek form here (εἰς τό + infinitive) can signal either purpose or result. It seems preferable, in this context, to use the relation of result, since it is clear from 2:10 that they actually were deceived by the man of sin.

Because of the use of the article, because of the use of the same Greek word as in 2:9, and because of the overall topic of the man of sin's appearance, τῷ ψεύδει 'the lie' (which they believe) is understood to refer to the false claims, the spurious miracles, etc., of the man of sin. In particular, it may well refer back to 2:4, where he actually claims to be God, the supremely false claim.

2:12 in order that everyone who did not believe the true *message* but who gladly chose *to be doing* what is wicked will be *justly* condemned *by God*. This verse gives God's ultimate purpose in his act of judgment described in 2:11b. The use of πάντες or ἅπαντες 'all' broadens the reference, however, to all who, whether in the time of the man of sin or not, reject the truth and love unrighteousness.

The two propositions which identify "everyone" are presented grammatically in negative and positive form:

> they did not believe the truth,
> they delighted in the wickedness.

BOUNDARIES AND COHERENCE

The boundaries of this unit have already been discussed under boundaries and coherence of 2:6–8 and 2:1–2. (It is interesting to note that this paragraph is introduced by a relative clause restating the main topic.)

Coherence is shown by the information relating to two topics—the main topic of 2:3b–12, viz., the revealing of the man of sin (2:9–10a), and a subtopic, those who are/will be perishing, introduced at the end of 2:10 and commented on in 2:10b–12.

Words relating to deception are found throughout the four verses: ψεῦδος 'a lie, fake' (2:9, 11); ἀπάτη 'deception' (2:10); and πλάνη 'delusion, error' (2:11). Note also the contrast with ἡ ἀλήθεια 'the truth' (2:10, 12).

There is also a group of words relating to evil and its judgment: Σατανᾶς 'Satan' (2:9); ἀδικία 'unrighteousness, wickedness' (2:10, 12); ἀπολλυμένοι 'being destroyed' (2:10); and κρίνω 'judge, condemn' (2:12).

PROMINENCE AND THEME

The main information in this paragraph is contained in the first clause, which runs from 2:9 through 10a, and to which the other clauses are subordinated. It consists of a subject οὗ...ἡ παρουσία 'whose presence', the verb ἐστιν 'is', and a complement consisting of three prepositional phrases: κατά 'according to...', ἐν 'accompanied by...', and καὶ ἐν... 'and accompanied by...'. What is prominent? Since reference to the subtopic "those who are perishing" is introduced in connection with the last of these phrases, it is considered to be prominent. This is supported by the fact that the main event in the corresponding proposition (2:10a) is "to deceive," and it is against being deceived that Paul warns the Thessalonians in the nucleus paragraph of this paragraph cluster. (The Greek is ἀπάτη here in 2:10a; ἐξαπατάω in 2:3a.)

Note that since the topic is an event "the lawless man will be present," the theme consists of the topic proposition and a comment proposition stating his main activity when he is present.

SECTION CONSTITUENT 2:13-14 (Paragraph: grounds for 2:15)

THEME: God chose you and summoned you in order that you should be saved and glorified.

RELATIONAL STRUCTURE	CONTENTS
orienter/result — RESULT	2:13a *Our(inc)* brothers, who are loved by *our(inc)* Lord *Jesus Christ*, we(exc) thank God very frequently for you,
└ reason	2:13b *because* we(exc) ought *to thank God for you*.
CONTENT/REASON₁ — MEANS	2:13c *We(exc) thank God* that/because God chose you from the beginning *of time*
└ purpose - RESULT	2:13d in order that *you* might be saved *by God*
├ means₁	2:13e by means of *the Holy* Spirit's setting *you* apart *for God*
└ means₂	2:13f and by means of *your* believing the true *message*.
┌ purpose	2:14a *And we(exc) thank God that/because* in order that this (2:13d-f) *might happen*
CONTENT/REASON₂ — MEANS	2:14b he summoned you by means of our(exc) *proclaiming* the good news *to you*
└ purpose	2:14c in order that *you* might be glorified like our(inc) Lord Jesus Christ is glorified.

NOTES

2:13a-b *Our(inc)* brothers, who are loved by *our(inc)* Lord *Jesus Christ*, we(exc) thank God very frequently [HYP] for you, *because* we(exc) ought *to thank God for you*. There are three interesting questions that arise in connection with these first two propositions and the clause representing them.

What is the significance of the particle δέ? The commentators are divided between (a) signaling the switch to a new topic, and (b) signaling a contrast between 2:13-14, and the preceding material. Clearly, there is the introduction of a new topic, and δέ signals this as it does frequently in this epistle. But is there a contrast? Those who say yes are divided between two possible contrasts:

1. Between "we" (which is represented by a forefronted free pronoun) and those "who are perishing," etc., in 2:10-12; or
2. Between the "salvation" emphasis of 2:13-14, and the "deceit, wickedness, and condemnation" emphasis of 2:10-13.

For the first, see the following paragraph. For the second, there is undoubtedly a general contrast in the lexical items used, so it could be that the δέ also correlates with that. But the transition to a new topic (and semantic unit) is more clearcut.

Why is there a forefronted ἡμεῖς 'we'? The usual explanation is that it is in contrast with "those who are perishing," the topic of 2:10-12. But if there were such a contrast, it would be between "you," who are described as chosen, called, and saved, and "those who are perishing." So the relation of contrast is implausible. It seems better, therefore, to say that Paul is resuming his "we-you" discourse framework, having departed from it for quite a number of verses in his discussion of the man of sin. So the ἡμεῖς is analyzed as essentially resumptive.

What is the significance of ὀφείλομεν 'we ought'? This has already been discussed in connection with 1:3b. Suffice it to say here, that unlike 1:3b, it precedes the infinitive εὐχαριστεῖν 'to thank', which may reflect the fact that (a) the thanking is less prominent here than in 1:3-4; and (b) the content of/ reason for the thanksgiving has shifted from the Thessalonians' faith and love, to God's choice and calling of them. The general contrast between the Thessalonians' spiritual state and that of those deceived by the man of sin could well be a third factor. Hence, ὀφείλομεν 'we ought' is handled as a separate proposition (2:13b), as a reason (of subjective obligation, as in 1:3b) for the thanksgiving.

2:13c *We(exc) thank God* that/because God chose you from the beginning *of time* There is a textual variant in this verse. The display follows the text which is preferred by the majority of commentators on the two grounds that it is more strongly supported by the manuscripts and it is collocationally more appropriate. This reading is ἀπ' ἀρχῆς 'from (the) beginning'; the alternative reading is ἀπαρχήν 'firstfruits'. It is pointed out by the commentators that "from the beginning" is collocationally suitable to "God chose/elected," whereas "firstfruits" is never used in that connection. Further, in Paul's six uses of ἀπαρχήν 'firstfruits' the noun is always qualified by a genitive (the apparent exception of 1 Cor. 15:23 is because the genitive is assumed implicitly from 15:20); and, in any case, it never refers to a local Christian congregation (or the church-universal either). In Rom. 8:23 it refers to the Holy Spirit; Rom. 11:16, to the Jews; Rom. 16:5, to an individual believer (the first convert); 1 Cor. 14:20 and 23 refer to Christ (first risen from the dead); and 1 Cor. 16:15, to a household of believers (first converts in Asia). Hence, ἀπαρχήν 'firstfruits' is rejected in favor of ἀπ' ἀρχῆς 'from (the) beginning)'. It is understood that this means "from the beginning of time," which, in this context, is equivalent to "in eternity."

2:13d-e in order that *you* might be saved *by God* by means of *the Holy* Spirit's setting *you* apart *for God* The only question here is what the meaning of the abstract noun ἁγιασμός is. Is it "sanctification," i.e., making holy; or "consecration," i.e., setting apart for God? Two factors favor the second of these alternatives:

1. The context is that of God's decisive acts, i.e., "chose" (2:13) and "called/summoned" (2:14), with purposes and means added. It suits the context better, therefore, to speak of the decisive act of the Spirit "setting apart" the one God has chosen.
2. Propositions 2:13e and 13f are conjoined, and a number of commentators draw attention to the order, which generally puzzles them, as one would expect the process of sanctification to follow, not precede, "faith in the truth," i.e., believing the gospel. But the initial work of the Spirit, it is widely agreed, precedes faith. The order, then, suggests that an initial decisive act is in mind, not a process.

The noun ἁγιασμός is used ten times in the New Testament, but 1 Pet. 1:2 is the only other case in which it is qualified by πνεύματος 'of the Spirit'. It is very likely that it has the same sense of "setting apart" in Peter also, where it is again associated with God's election.

If the view is taken that ἁγιασμός means "the process of sanctification," then 2:13e would read "by means of *the Holy* Spirit causing that *you* should be/become holy."

2:13f and by means of *your* believing the true message. Note the same use of "truth" here as in 2:10 and 12 above. In particular, 2:12a is very similar (apart from the negation) and the similarity should be retained in the translation.

2:14a *And we(exc) thank God that/because* in order that this (2:13d-f) might happen The Greek is simply εἰς ὅ 'to which' or 'for which purpose'. It is very widely agreed that this εἰς ὅ phrase refers back to the phrases in the preceding clause which also begin with εἰς and which are represented by 2:13d-f. As is argued under prominence and theme, εἰς ὅ is regarded as an anaphoric repetition of these phrases so as to introduce further statements related to them.

2:14b he summoned you by means of our(exc) *proclaiming* the good news *to you* The Greek verb ἐκάλεσεν is very widely translated "called." However, this can be misleading for a translator, so "summoned" has been substituted to try to convey the ideas of (a) authority and (b) effectiveness, both of which components are involved in the Pauline use of this verb when God is the agent (cf. the use of the cognate abstract noun κλῆσις 'call/summon' in 1:11).

2:14c in order that *you* might be glorified like our(inc) Lord Jesus Christ is glorified. The noun περιποίησις has the meaning "possession (of), acquisition (of), obtaining (of)," but, if it is represented by any of these verbs, there are problems in this context; "in order that you should possess, acquire, obtain the glory of our Lord Jesus Christ" tends to give the impression that it is taken from him. Rather, the idea is that they would come to have such glory as the Lord himself has. It is best, therefore, to treat περιποίησιν δόξης 'acquisition of (the) glory' as semantically equivalent to "be glorified." The following genitive construction τοῦ κυρίου ἡμῶν Ἰησοῦ Χριστοῦ 'of our Lord Jesus Christ' is then expressed semantically as a comparison "like our Lord Jesus Christ is glorified."

BOUNDARIES AND COHERENCE

Verse 2:13 is marked as unit-initial by the occurrence of the particle δέ, the vocative ἀδελφοί 'brothers', and a new performative ὀφείλομεν εὐχαριστεῖν τῷ θεῷ 'we ought to thank God'.

It is also marked by the change from the third person orientation of 2:7-12 (or the second and third person orientation of 2:3-12) to the first person plural and second person plural of 2:13-14.

There is also a change of topic from the appearing of the man of sin to thanksgiving for the salvation of the Thessalonians.

However, while a new unit clearly starts with 2:13, its ending is more problematical. Many versions and commentaries treat 2:13-15 as a unit. There is good evidence, however, to treat 2:15 as starting a new unit (for details, see boundaries and coherence for 2:15).

Verses 2:13 and 14 are bound together by the "salvation" terminology used—in fact, some writers see these verses as a theological system in miniature. The terminology consists of the following: ἠγαπημένοι 'beloved' (from ἀγαπάω 'to love'), εἵλατο 'chose' (from αἱρέομαι 'to choose), σωτηρίαν 'salvation', ἁγιασμῷ 'sanctification, consecration, πίστει 'faith', ἀληθείας 'truth', ἐκάλεσεν 'called, summoned', and δόξης 'glory'. Note, also, references to the Trinity as God *the Father*, the Lord *Jesus Christ*, and the Spirit.

PROMINENCE AND THEME

Reaching conclusions concerning the prominence structure of these verses, and consequently, deciding on the theme, is not at all easy. There are two basic questions:

1. What is the prominence relation between the performative "we thank God" and the content of or reasons for that performative, introduced by the ὅτι 'that/because' in 2:13?
2. What is the prominence relation between 2:13c and 14b, i.e., the two main statements within the material introduced by ὅτι 'that/because'?

These two issues are discussed below.

Formally, the performative in 2:13 is very similar to that in 1:3. In the discussion of the theme for 1:3-4, it was argued that the performative "we(exc) thank God" was equally prominent with the content/reason it was related to. In the display for this paragraph, the performative proposition is regarded as of lesser prominence than the content/reason propositions. Why is this? There are (at least) three factors that have influenced this decision:

1. Normally, "we thank" performatives are found in the introduction to the body of an epistle—but 2:13 is clearly not that; it is not part of the "interpersonal" introduction, but simply part of a grounds paragraph within the hortatory matters of the epistle.
2. When such performatives as "we thank" occur in Paul's epistles, in most case Paul thanks God for the spiritual life of the recipients themselves—their faith, love, endurance, hope, etc. Here he is thanking God for what God has done for them.
3. Tied up with both the preceding points is the fact that the next unit (2:15) is a conclusion, in the form of a command, based (in part) on the content of this paragraph. But the exhortation is not based on Paul's thanking God, but on what God has done for the Thessalonians, i.e., it is an exhortation addressed to them in the light of 2:13b-14, i.e., from the ὅτι 'that/because' onwards.

It is concluded, therefore, that the content/reason outranks the performative in this particular context.

The opening clause of the content/reason material reads ὅτι εἵλατο ὑμᾶς ὁ θεὸς ἀπ' ἀρχῆς 'that God chose you from the beginning'. The only other finite verb is in the first clause in 2:14, εἰς ὃ [καὶ] ἐκάλεσεν ὑμᾶς 'to which he [also] called you. Is this second finite verb, or more strictly, the proposition it represents, of equal rank with the proposition represented by the first? So far as I can see, it depends on how εἰς ὃ 'to which' is analyzed. If it is regarded as a repetition (in anaphoric form) of the material that follows ἀπ' ἀρχῆς 'from the beginning' for the purpose of clarification or prominence, then it would normally be treated as having the relation of equivalence, and of lower rank than the first statement. If, however, as seems to be the majority opinion, it is a repetition of the material following ἀπ' ἀρχῆς so that Paul could add further dependent clauses to it, then it is simply a grammatical device to avoid a complete repetition of the whole clause, and εἰς ὃ would represent a repetition of εἰς σωτηρίαν... 'to salvation...' of the same rank as what it repeats. It is this viewpoint that is reflected in the display, so that there are two main (conjoined) propositions in the content, and so the theme uses both. The two statements "God chose you" and "God summoned (= called) you" are not synonymous. It is explicitly stated that the act of choosing was before time; the calling came with the proclamation of the gospel. The choosing in eternity is put into effect by the "calling" in time, and both are necessary for salvation, etc.

There is, however, one other question in connection with the theme. Should it be given in the simple form "God chose you and summoned you" or should it also state what the purposes of these actions were? It seems preferable to state the purposes explicitly, as, in any case, they would be implied by the theme, since the choosing and summoning have to be for some purpose; they are semantically "incomplete" without their purposes. The theme, therefore, consists of the propositional cluster 2:13c–d, conjoined with the propositional cluster 2:14b–c.

SECTION CONSTITUENT 2:15 (Propositional Cluster: Nucleus of 2:1–17)

THEME: *Continue believing the body of teaching which was committed to you by us(exc).*	
RELATIONAL STRUCTURE	CONTENTS
┌─ contraction	2:15a Therefore, *our(exc)* brothers, continue to be firm *concerning what you believe*;
NUCLEUS ─ NUCLEUS	2:15b that is, continue believing the body of *true* teaching
└─ identification ─ RESULT	2:15c which was committed to you *by us(exc)*
of 'teaching' ├─ means₁	2:15d by means of our(exc) speaking *to you*
└─ means₂	2:15e and by means of our(exc)/my *writing* a letter *to you*.

NOTES

2:15a Therefore, *our(exc)* brothers, continue to be firm *concerning what you believe*; The initial "therefore" represents two Greek particles, ἄρα οὖν. While it is clear that a (hortatory) conclusion is being introduced, two questions can be asked about this sequence of particles:

1. How do they differ from the single use of ἄρα, and the single use of οὖν—particularly the latter?
2. On what grounds is the hortatory conclusion based?

Neither of these questions is at all easy to answer. According to Moulton and Geden's Concordance (1957), Paul is the only New Testament author to use ἄρα οὖν, and he does so twelve times in all—eight times in Romans and four times elsewhere. Οὖν, outside the combination of ἄρα οὖν, he uses about a hundred times, whereas ἄρα, other than in ἄρα οὖν, he uses only fifteen times. It seems reasonable, then, to ask the question in the form: What difference does adding ἄρα to οὖν make, compared with using οὖν on its own? Or, putting it another way: Why did Paul choose ἄρα οὖν here rather than the much more common οὖν? No independent research has been done, but Giblin (1967:43) states: "When ἄρα οὖν, introduces a hortative conclusion (as here and in Rom. 8:12; Rom 14:12–19; Gal. 6:10; 1 Thess. 5:6) the predominant character of the preceding section or context is also hortative, notwithstanding a certain amount of exposition or argumentation at time." He also speaks of "the conclusive force of ἄρα οὖν, with regard to all that precedes in ch. 2" (see the following discussion).

There are broadly three possible answers to the second question. The exhortation in 2:15 is based on 2:13–14 only; or on 2:1–14; or on all of chapters 1 and 2 so far. That it is based at least on 2:13–14 all are agreed, and it may be that the ἄρα links 2:13–14 to 2:15 closely. But does 2:15 look beyond that? There are three good reasons for thinking 2:1–12 are in mind also:

1. The verb used, στήκετε 'stand firm', is an antonym of σαλευθῆναι 'to be upset, shaken' used in 2:2.
2. The second command refers to 'holding firmly to what they had been taught, and 2:1–12 reminds them of what they had been taught, as opposed to the false teaching that had arisen.
3. False messages and letters, purporting to be from Paul (and his associates) are referred to in 2:2; genuine messages and letter(s) are referred to in 2:15.

Hence, there is good evidence to link 2:15 with 2:1–14.

But how about chapter 1? The main argument in favor of basing 2:15 on all of chapters 1 and 2 is that στήκετε 'stand firm' is seen as an appropriate exhortation in the light of the persecutions they were undergoing, which are referred to in chapter 1. There are three objections to this view:

1. There is no suggestion that they were not standing firm, indeed Paul commends their steadfastness.
2. It seems likely that στήκετε is not used in the context of persecution (see note in paragraph below).
3. Chapter 1 is the introduction of the body of the letter, and it does not seem logical to ground an exhortation on introductory material.

Hence, it is concluded that the command in 2:15 is related to 2:1–14. (See also the discussion of the boundaries and coherence of 2:1–17.)

What does στήκετε 'keep standing' mean, and how is this command related to the following one? Clearly, στήκετε is being used figuratively—the Thessalonian believers are not being exhorted to remain in a standing position, like soldiers on parade! Apart from John 8:44, only Paul uses it figuratively. Three collocations can be distinguished:

1. + dative, as in Rom. 14:4;
2. + ἐν 'in', as in 1 Cor. 16:13 (in the faith), Phil. 1:27 (in one spirit), 4:1 (in the Lord), 1 Thess. 3:8 (also in the Lord); and
3. absolutely, as in Gal. 5:1 and the present passage.

The example in Galatians is very similar to that being considered here, as it is an imperative + οὖν. There Paul says, "For freedom Christ has freed you; stand, therefore, and do not again be subject to the yoke of slavery." In this context, it seems likely that "stand" means "continue to be free, remain in your freedom," and that the negative command is a restatement for emphasis. (It is clear that persecution has no relevance to the command in Galatians.)

A similar analysis is proposed here, namely, that στήκετε is equivalent to a generic command "remain firm in your beliefs," and that the second command spells this out again in somewhat more detail. This means that the καί 'and' is regarded as "epexegetical," i.e., explaining what the previous statement said.

2:15b that is, continue believing the body of *true* teaching Again, a figurative expression is found in the command. Κρατεῖτε, in its primary sense, is "to hold on to (something)," usually people. Here, however, it is collocated with παραδόσεις 'teachings' (see the following paragraph for further discussion). The nonfigurative meaning would, therefore, be something like "continue believing," "continue accepting as true," "do not abandon," etc.

The formal object of "hold on to" is παραδόσεις, usually translated "traditions." In the gospels it refers to the accumulated extra-Biblical teachings of the Pharisees, for which Jesus condemned them. But in the epistles it refers to the body of teaching passed on by the apostles and committed to them by the Lord. It is very difficult to reflect these components in a display; "the body of (true) teaching which was committed to you" is an attempt to do so. The teaching would cover both doctrine and behavior.

2:15c–e which was committed to you *by us(exc) by means of our(exc) speaking to you* and by means of our(exc)/my *writing* a letter *to you*. This proposition identifies which "body of teaching" Paul was referring to, and the following means propositions are related to this identification proposition; they state how the body of teaching was communicated to the Thessalonian believers.

BOUNDARIES AND COHERENCE

Verse 2:15 is marked as unit-initial by the occurrence of the vocative ἀδελφοί 'brothers' and the particles ἄρα οὖν 'therefore'.

There is also a switch from expository genre to hortatory genre.

There is a change of topic from what God has done for the Thessalonians to commands to the Thessalonians not to depart from what they have been taught.

Verse 2:16 is analyzed as the start of a new unit—see the discussion in connection with 2:16-17.

This unit, only a propositional cluster in composition, formally consists of two present tense commands linked by καί 'and'. The unit, therefore, has a number of "you(pl)" references; the three verbs στήκετε 'stand', κρατεῖτε 'hold on to', and ἐδιδάχθητε 'you were taught', and the vocative noun ἀδελφοί '(you) brothers'.

PROMINENCE AND THEME

Formally, there are two independent finite verbs, linked by καί 'and'; so the question arises as to whether they are semantically conjoined and of equal rank, or not. This issue is discussed in the notes in connection with 2:15a. There it is suggested that the first verb στήκετε 'continue standing' is semantically a contraction of κρατεῖτε τὰς παραδόσεις ἃς ἐδιδάχθητε 'hold on to the teachings which you were taught', but put in figurative form. The second command, represented by 2:15b, is regarded, therefore, as the nucleus proposition of this propositional cluster, and hence, as the theme of this short unit.

SECTION CONSTITUENT 2:16–17 (Paragraph: means of 2:15)

THEME: We(exc) pray that our(inc) Lord Jesus Christ himself will encourage you and cause you to continue doing and speaking what is good.

RELATIONAL STRUCTURE	CONTENTS
ORIENTER — NUCLEUS	2:16a *We(exc) pray to* our(inc) Lord Jesus Christ himself—and to God, our(inc) Father—
description₁ of 'Jesus'	2:16b who loved us(inc)
RESULT₁	2:16c and who encouraged us(inc) forever
description₂ of 'Jesus' — RESULT₂	2:16d and who caused us(inc) to confidently expect the good things *God has promised to give to us(inc)*
means	2:16e by means of *our(inc) Lord Jesus Christ* acting graciously *toward us(inc)*;
CONTENT₁	2:17a *we(exc) pray that* our(inc) Lord Jesus Christ will encourage you
CONTENT₂	2:17b and *that* he will cause *you* to continue doing every *sort of* good deed and to continue speaking everything that is good.

NOTES

2:16a *We(exc) pray to* our(inc) Lord Jesus Christ himself—and to God, our(inc) Father— The performative "we(exc) pray" is implied by the use of the optative mood. "We(exc)" is probably the better alternative exegetically, as "we(exc)" is used very widely in this epistle, and there is no reason to suppose Paul would have excluded Silas and Timothy from the implied performative (cf. also 1:11 προσευχόμεθα 'we(exc) pray').

2:16b who loved us(inc) "Loved" is expressed by an aorist participle (ἀγαπήσας), not the more common perfect (cf. 2:13). This use of the aorist might be better represented in English by "set his love upon us" or "showed his love to us." This latter is the sense most commonly referred to in the commentaries. Because of the prominence given to the Lord Jesus Christ in this prayer, the descriptions given in 2:16 are considered to refer to him, rather than to the Father, which is the nearest referent. It is true, love for us is usually associated with the Father, but in 2:13, just a few verses previously, Paul has described the Thessalonians as loved by the Lord Jesus.

2:16c and who encouraged us(inc) forever The abstract noun παράκλησις is used here, and as always with various forms of this root it is difficult to decide what translation to give it in English—comfort, encouragement, exhortation, and sometimes beseeching. In this context "encouragement" seems the most appropriate; all that our Lord Jesus has done for us is an encouragement to all his people throughout time and eternity, no matter what their circumstances, but especially to those who are undergoing persecution, since he, too, suffered persecution at the hands of his enemies.

2:16d–e and who caused us(inc) to confidently expect the good things *God has promised to give to us(inc)* by means of *our(inc) Lord Jesus Christ* acting graciously *toward us(inc)*; The Greek for 2:16d says δοὺς...ἐλπίδα ἀγαθήν 'and gave good hope'. Ἐλπίς 'hope' in the New Testament is a complex noun, probably best spelled out as "confidently expecting what God has promised to give us." But what does ἀγαθήν 'good' add? It is hard to say, but it could refer either to the good basis for our Christian hope (i.e., it is a "sure and certain" hope), or to the quality of what we look forward to; all that God has promised us is good. It is this latter view which is represented in the display, but the former would be quite acceptable exegetically.

2:17a *we(exc) pray that* our(inc) Lord Jesus Christ will encourage you The verb corresponding to the noun παράκλησιν 'encouragement' used in 2:16c is used here, and is also translated by "encourage." The object of the verb is ὑμῶν τὰς καρδίας 'your hearts', and this is taken to mean "inwardly," i.e., in their thinking, their emotions, their will. However, while the emphasis is on the inward aspect of encouragement, it is still the

Thessalonians who are being encouraged, so only "you" is used in the display.

2:17b and *that* he will cause *you* to continue doing every *sort of* good deed and to continue speaking everything that is good. The only question of interest in connection with this proposition is how the verb στηρίζω is to be represented in the display. Most versions use "strengthen" or "establish," which gives the impression to an English speaker that the Thessalonians were weak or unstable (in the light of what follows) in what they said and did. The verb is used figuratively ten times in the New Testament; and Luke, in Acts, uses the very similar compound form ἐπιστηρίζω. A study of its use in these passages yields the sense "cause someone to continue (in some state/activity)". The "someone" is expressed in the accusative case, and "in some state/activity" is generally carried implicitly in the context. In most contexts it has the general sense of causing (usually in connection with exhortation and encouragement, as here) some group of believers to continue steadfastly following the Lord. The presupposition underlying its use seems to be that the Christian life is not easy, and στηρίζω is addressed to that fact. Sometimes, as here, the agent is God or the Lord Jesus (Rom. 16:24; 1 Thess. 3:13; 2 Thess. 3:3). More commonly, the agent is leaders among the Lord's people (Luke 22:32 (Peter); all the Acts passages; Rom. 1:11 (Paul); 1 Thess. 3:2 (Timothy)). Sometimes the agents are the recipients themselves (Jas. 5:8; Rev. 3:2). (The example in 2 Pet. 1:12 has no expressed agent.)

The collocation here with ἐν παντὶ ἔργῳ καὶ λόγῳ ἀγαθῷ 'in every good deed and word' supports the meaning "cause to continue/maintain." In spite of persecution, in spite of false teaching, in spite of the idleness of some, and in spite of Paul's absence, they were to maintain a consistent Christian walk. So Paul prays here that the Lord would enable them to do this.

BOUNDARIES AND COHERENCE

In 2:16 there is the particle δέ, a change of subject, and a change of subgenre from exhortation (command) to prayer (shown by a switch from the imperative to the optative mood), and this combination clearly marks the start of a new semantic unit.

Verse 2:17 coincides with the end of section 2:1–17 (for further discussion, see boundaries and coherence of 2:1–17).

Grammatically, 2:16–17 is one sentence, with a compound, forefronted subject and two conjoined verbs. There is also a limited amount of lexical parallelism: παράκλησιν 'encouragement' in 2:16 and παρακαλέσαι 'may he encourage' in 2:17; and ἀγαθήν 'good' in 2:16, with αγαθῷ 'good' in 2:17.

PROMINENCE AND THEME

In this paragraph, prominence turns out to be unusually interesting. The problem that all exegetes face is that this sentence has a *compound* subject—our Lord Jesus Christ *and* God our Father—but a *singular* verb: "may he encourage and strengthen." How is this to be explained?

The general answer of the commentators is that, since Paul thought of the Lord Jesus and the Father as one God, he used singular verb forms, even though this violated the normal grammatical concord of number between subject and verb. It would be an unusual case of the *constructio ad sensum*, i.e., a grammatical construction in which semantic considerations override grammatical ones. The best known example of this in the New Testament is referring to the Holy Spirit by the masculine pronoun αὐτός, even though the noun for spirit is neuter, requiring the form αὐτό. It is difficult to reflect this analysis in a display in English, as this *constructio ad sensum* is not allowed in English, so 2:17a and 17b would have to use "they" rather than "he."

It is possible, however, to posit an alternative analysis of the data which does not require the assumption of a *constructio ad sensum*. Along with the fact that the verbs used are singular, the commentators very widely note that this is one of the relatively rare occasions in which reference to the Lord Jesus is placed *before* reference to the Father in this type of compound construction. Further, the emphatic pronoun αὐτός 'himself' is used with the Lord Jesus, and he is given the fullest possible title "our Lord Jesus Christ." It is hard, therefore, to avoid the conclusion that Paul was using a variety of devices to give prominence to the Lord Jesus in this prayer. Furthermore, there are two very similar prayers, expressed by means of the optative mood, in 3:5 and 3:16. In both of these prayers, it is the Lord Jesus who is referred to, without reference to the Father at all. In addition, the full title, using "Lord," "Jesus," and "Christ" occurs about sixty-six times in Paul's epistles, in various orders. But this threefold title is used three times more often in 2 Thessalonians than in any other epistle (ignoring Philemon because of its shortness).

The conclusion, then, is that this is an epistle in which special prominence is given to the Lord Jesus, and this prominence is very clear in 2:16. Hence, it is also concluded, the verbs are singular because the (prominent) subject is the Lord Jesus Christ. The Father is closely associated with him in the prayer, but with less prominence semantically. This has no *theological* significance—such a conclusion would be totally erroneous. It simply reflects the fact that Paul, in this letter to the Thessalonians, felt it necessary to lay considerable emphasis on the Lord Jesus. This ability to give prominence to one half of a compound construction is found in English also, and is used in the display.

With this approach, the theme statement refers only to the Lord Jesus Christ, and not to the Father.

DIVISION CONSTITUENT 3:1–5 (Section: conjoined to 2:1–17 and 3:6–16a)

THEME: Pray that more and more people will believe the message about our(inc) Lord Jesus. Our(inc) Lord Jesus will cause you to continue to be steadfast and he will protect you from the evil one.

RELATIONAL STRUCTURE	CONTENTS
NUCLEUS$_1$	3:1–2 Pray that more and more people will believe the message about our(inc) Lord Jesus.
NUCLEUS$_2$	3:3–5 Our(inc) Lord Jesus will cause you to continue to be steadfast and he will protect you from the evil one.

BOUNDARIES AND COHERENCE

Verse 3:1 shows the three initial marks of a section, but in modified form; the vocative, ἀδελφοί 'brothers' is the same, but the performative is replaced by a direct command προσεύχεσθε...περὶ ἡμῶν 'pray...for us', and the usual conjunction δέ is replaced by τὸ λοιπόν 'as for the rest'. Verse 3:5 is a prayer and is analyzed as a section closure feature, as with 1:11–12, and 2:16–17 in the preceding sections. In addition, 3:6 shows section-initial boundary signals. The use of παραγγέλλομεν 'we command' in 3:4 and 6 can also be considered as a tail-head link. Hence, 3:1–5 is analyzed as a section, but, as was discussed in connection with the body as a whole, a section of lesser prominence than the two sections that flank it (2:1–17 and 3:6–16a).

The coherence of this unit is primarily referential—the commentators all mention the difficulty of perceiving any relational coherence. There are several types of referential coherence shown:

1. Referential repetition: this is primarily reference to "the Lord" in every verse, except 3:2; and to "you(pl)," again in every verse except 3:2. References to "we(exc)" are also found in 3:1, 2, and 4.
2. Tail-head lexical links:, πίστις 'faith' in 3:2 and πιστός 'faithful' in 3:3 (notice also the use of πονηρός 'evil' in both 3:2 and 3).
3. Semantically related words: in addition to πίστις 'faith' and πιστός 'faithful', there is also πεποίθαμεν 'we have confidence' in 3:4.

From the standpoint of relational coherence, 3:1 and 2 form one sentence, and are relationally tied together. Each of 3:3, 4, and 5 is introduced by δέ, signaling a transition from one topic/unit to another, and its frequency in so few verses underlines the lack of close relational links between the constituents of this section.

PROMINENCE AND THEME

This short section is analyzed as consisting of two paragraphs: 3:1–2 and 3–5. Verses 3:1–2 clearly form a unit, as they constitute Paul's request for prayer. the unity of 3:3–5 is much more problematical, and is discussed when that unit is treated later. Taking it as established here, the question still remains: How are these two paragraphs related to each other? There is no overt relational link, they are simply juxtaposed within a larger unit, and so are regarded as conjoined. Nor is it at all easy to decide on their relative prominence. Lacking any clear grounds for ranking one above the other, they are treated as of equal rank, and the theme consists of the two paragraph themes.

SECTION CONSTITUENT 3:1–2 (Paragraph: Nucleus₁ of 3:1–5)

THEME: Pray that more and more people will believe the message about our(inc) Lord Jesus.	
RELATIONAL STRUCTURE	CONTENTS
ORIENTER	3:1a As for the other matters, *our(inc)* brothers, pray for us(exc)
EXHORTATION₁ — GOAL — step	3:1b that more and more people will soon hear the message about *our(inc)* Lord *Jesus*
NUCLEUS	3:1c and that they will believe this message
comparison	3:1d just as you *are doing/have done*.
exhortation₂	3:2a And pray for us(exc) that we(exc) will be rescued from those people *here* who are perverse and evil.
grounds for exhortation₁	3:2b *Pray like this (3:1b-c) since not everyone believes this message about our(inc) Lord Jesus.*

NOTES

3:1a As for the other matters, *our(inc)* brothers, pray for us(exc) This section opens with the Greek words τὸ λοιπόν, generally translated "finally" in English versions. Moule (1960:161–2) suggests that the primary meaning of this phrase is "for what remains," and that it is used in several senses:

1. Temporally, meaning "from now on."
2. Logically, meaning "hence, so, therefore."
3. As an orienter "finally."

In English, however, "finally" carries the idea of being near the end too strongly, and τὸ λοιπόν is not always used close to the end, as in this case and in 1 Thess. 4:7. Rather, as some commentators suggest, it introduces the remaining matters of the epistle, without prejudice as to their length, and this sense also fits in better with Moule's analysis.

This sense of τὸ λοιπόν fits well here. The only problem with it is that Paul's requests for prayer for himself and his colleagues are generally much nearer the end of his letters, and are followed by such personal matters as news, greetings, etc. The rather disjointed nature of 3:1–5 is also characteristic of the end of a letter. However, since Paul goes on to deal with another major matter and does not turn to greetings, etc., the sense of "now, as for the remaining matters" is regarded as the most appropriate here. It is also difficult to decide whether τὸ λοιπόν refers only to this section, i.e., 3:1–5, or to this section and the following one, i.e., 3:6–16a, covering the rest of the body of the epistle. Since the next section is a well-developed section, and deals with a major disciplinary matter, τὸ λοιπόν is regarded as relevant to this section only.

3:1b–c that more and more people will soon hear the message about *our(inc)* Lord *Jesus* and that they will believe this message The Greek underlying these two propositions is ἵνα ὁ λόγος τοῦ κυρίου τρέχῃ καὶ δοξάζηται 'that the message of the Lord would run and be glorified'. Both of these are unusual collocations, and need further discussion.

Two ideas are suggested for ὁ λόγος τοῦ κυρίου τρέχῃ 'the message of the Lord would run'. One is that it might spread rapidly, the other is that it might do so *without hindrance*; and some suggest both. The latter view is rejected on the grounds that Paul knew, both from teaching and experience, that the spread of the gospel would always meet with hindrances and opposition, as it was doing in both Thessalonica and Corinth, so he is hardly likely to ask for prayer that it would not meet with hindrances. However, prayer for its rapid spread is, in effect, a prayer that whatever hindrances there were would be overcome, and not prove successful.

In some languages, it may be collocationally acceptable to use an expression such as "the message of the Lord will spread rapidly." But, for those where "the message of the Lord" cannot be the subject, the display uses the propositional form "that more and more people will soon hear the message."

What does ὁ λόγος τοῦ κυρίου...δοξάζηται 'that the message of the Lord would be glorified' mean? It is generally agreed that it means to honor the message as it should be honored, being a message of salvation from God. Paul's own description of how the Thessalonians had received the message is the best description of its meaning: "the message of God...you accepted it not as the message of men but as what it really is, the message of God" (1 Thess. 2:13). Hence, in effect, it means to accept or believe the message—no other response can "glorify" it.

Propositions 3:1b and 1c are considered to be in the relation of step-goal, i.e., that it is necessary for people to hear the gospel before they can believe it.

3:1d just as you *are doing/have done*. The Greek says simply καθὼς καὶ πρὸς ὑμᾶς 'just as also among you'. Two brief comments:

It is not clear, since no verb is expressed, whether Paul is referring to the initial reception of the gospel by the Thessalonians, or to its continued successful spread among them. The main verbs are both present tense, so this probably favors the second of these alternatives.

In the display, this proposition is related only to 3:1c. But it is collocationally acceptable with both verbs, so it could also be related to 3:1b. If the argument in favor of 3:1c being the more prominent is valid, this might slightly favor 3:1d being related to 3:1c only, rather than to both 3:1c and b.

3:2a And pray for us(exc) that we(exc) will be rescued from those people *here* who are perverse and evil. The Greek adjective translated in the display by "perverse" is ἄτοπος. It is a relatively unusual word, and probably carries the implication here of deliberate obstinacy, shutting one's eyes to the facts. Phillips and the Jerusalem Bible translate it by "bigoted" and the NEB by "wrongheaded" (see also the note in the paragraph below).

It is widely agreed by the commentators that the use of the aorist tense for "be rescued," and the article with "perverse and evil men" implies that (a) a specific time of opposition is being referred to, rather than a general request (like those in 3:1), and (b) it was probably known to the Thessalonians. It is commonly considered that it refers to Jewish opposition to Paul and the gospel message in Corinth (ἄτοπος is considered to be particularly appropriate to unbelieving Jews).

3:2b *Pray like this* (3:1b–c) since not everyone believes *this message about our(inc) Lord Jesus*. The γάρ 'for' clause can be related to what precedes it in two different ways. It can give a reason for the perverseness and wickedness of the persecutors; or it can be related to the nucleus, and give grounds for Paul's request that the gospel would spread and be believed. Although it is difficult to find objective reasons for choosing one or the other, the latter probably accords better with the use of γάρ, but either would be quite acceptable in a translation.

BOUNDARIES AND COHERENCE

The initial boundary coincides with that of section 3:1–5 (see discussion there).

A break between 3:2 and 3 is posited because:

1. There is a change from a request for prayer (3:1–2) to a statement about the Lord. That is to say, the "we(exc)–you" orientation is changed for a "the Lord–you" orientation.
2. Verses 3:1–2 form an obviously relationally coherent unit, and the relational chain is broken between 3:2 and 3.
3. Verse 3:3 has the conjunction δέ.
4. There is a tail-head link of πίστις 'faith' πιστός 'faithful' (and perhaps πονηρῶν 'evil(pl)' with πονηροῦ 'evil(sg)') between 3:2 and 3.

PROMINENCE AND THEME

Basically, this paragraph consists of an orienter, in the form of a command "pray for us," together with its content. The content consists of two conjoined halves, one being a request for the successful spread of the gospel, the other a request for deliverance for Paul and his associates from the danger that threatened them. Of the two requests, the first is considered the more prominent for the following reasons:

1. It refers to "the Lord," and "the Lord" is not only a motif in this section, but in the epistle as a whole.
2. Although the two halves are formally joined by καί 'and', it could be argued that the deliverance of Paul and his associates was a means to the end of the successful spread of the gospel. It would be only one of a number of means, but a means nonetheless. Hence, the first request is considered more important.
3. The fact that the request in 3:1 is, in fact, the first, may also indicate that it is the more important of the two requests.

However, the first request is formally in two parts also, as indicated by two verbs with the same formal categories (third person singular present subjunctive) being linked by καί 'and'. Again, it is suggested, from a thematic standpoint, that one of these is more important than the other. The first is clearly figurative in form, and is presupposed as a necessary means by the second: the first refers to the spread of the message, the second to its acceptance. Hence, the latter is considered the more prominent of the two, yielding the theme: "Pray that more and more people will believe the message about our(inc) Lord Jesus."

SECTION CONSTITUENT 3:3–5 (Paragraph: Nucleus₂ of 3:1–5)

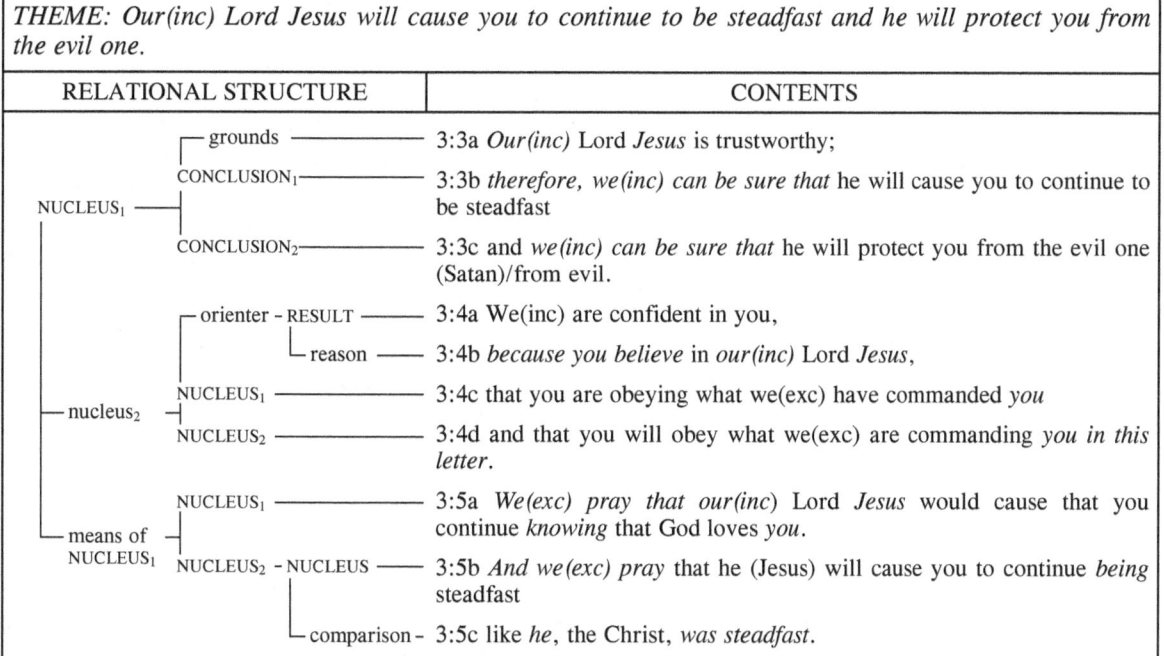

THEME: *Our(inc) Lord Jesus will cause you to continue to be steadfast and he will protect you from the evil one.*

RELATIONAL STRUCTURE	CONTENTS
NUCLEUS₁ — grounds / CONCLUSION₁	3:3a *Our(inc) Lord Jesus is trustworthy;*
	3:3b *therefore, we(inc) can be sure that* he will cause you to continue to be steadfast
CONCLUSION₂	3:3c and *we(inc) can be sure that* he will protect you from the evil one (Satan)/from evil.
nucleus₂ — orienter - RESULT	3:4a We(inc) are confident in you,
reason	3:4b *because you believe* in *our(inc) Lord Jesus,*
NUCLEUS₁	3:4c that you are obeying what we(exc) have commanded *you*
NUCLEUS₂	3:4d and that you will obey what we(exc) are commanding *you in this letter.*
means of NUCLEUS₁ — NUCLEUS₁	3:5a *We(exc) pray that our(inc)* Lord *Jesus* would cause that you continue *knowing* that God loves *you.*
NUCLEUS₂ - NUCLEUS	3:5b And *we(exc) pray* that he (Jesus) will cause you to continue *being* steadfast
comparison	3:5c like *he, the Christ, was steadfast.*

NOTES

3:3a-b *Our(inc) Lord Jesus is trustworthy; therefore, we(inc) can be sure that* **he will cause you to continue to be steadfast** The clause underlying proposition 3:3b is commonly translated "he will establish you" (fut. of στηρίζω). The verb στηρίζω has the primary sense of "to cause to stand." It is thus a causative form corresponding to στήκω 'to stand', used in 2:15 (see the discussion of 2:15a). It was argued there that, when στήκω is used figuratively, it meant "remain firm in...," where the blank is filled in from the surrounding context. What is the context here? Paul's request for prayer in 3:2, his (probable) reference to "the evil one" in this same verse, and the reference to "endurance" in 3:5 make it likely that the persecution the Thessalonians were undergoing was in Paul's mind at this point in the letter. Hence, the verb στηρίζω is taken to mean "cause (you) to remain steadfast" in this context.

3:3c and *we(inc) can be sure that* **he will protect you from the evil one (Satan)/from evil.** The last two words of this sentence may be translated as "the evil one" or "evil" (in a generic sense). They are formally ambiguous, the masculine and neuter genitive forms being identical. There is little in the way of evidence to decide. As pointed out in connection with 3:3b, there are several references to persecution in these five verses, which might favor the sense "the evil one." It has also been suggested that the emphasis on "the Lord" in these verses favors a personal interpretation here. On the other hand, the only other two collocations of φυλάσσω 'to guard/protect' and ἀπό 'from', found in Luke 12:15 and 1 Jn. 5:21, are with specific sins: greed or covetousness, and idols. This could support the sense of evil. With so little evidence one way or the other, the translator is free to choose.

3:4a–b We(exc) are confident in you, *because you believe* in *our(inc)* Lord Jesus, A literal translation of πεποίθαμεν...ἐν κυρίῳ ἐφ' ὑμᾶς is "we are confident in (the) Lord upon you." The question that arises is: In whom was Paul's confidence placed at this point—in the Lord, or in the Thessalonians? There are two closely related problems to be solved:

1. Can any explanation be offered for the different prepositions with which πεποίθαμεν 'we are confident' (and related forms) occurs?
2. What, in any case, is the meaning of "in (the) Lord"?

Paul uses the perfect tense of πείθω 'to persuade' some eighteen times in his epistles, and there is also a similar use in Heb. 6:9. A study of these yields the following conclusions:

1. The matter or content of the confidence, what it was about, is most commonly expressed by ὅτι with a following clause (as here), but it can be expressed by an accusative and infinitive construction (e.g., Rom. 2:19), or by an accusative phrase (Phil. 1:6, 25), or by a dative phrase (Phlm. 21).
2. Ἐπί or εἰς with the accusative case refers to the persons "with respect to whom" there is confidence that they can, or will, do something, e.g., 2 Cor. 1:9 (God, not ourselves); Gal. 5:10 (you).
3. Περί with the genitive case refers to the person/s about whose present state confidence is expressed—e.g., Rom. 15:14 ("that you are full of goodness"); Heb. 6:9 ("that you possess better things/states connected with salvation").
4. Ἐν with the dative is the most difficult. It seems to mean "in connection with." It is used in Phil. 3:3–4 three times in the phrase ἐν σαρκί 'in (connection with the) flesh'. It defines the topic of the matter of confidence—all the examples Paul goes on to give in that passage are aspects of "the flesh," i.e., natural Jewish advantages which he had.

If this analysis is correct, then in this verse the matter of Paul's confidence is that the Thessalonians are obeying and will obey what he has said; and his confidence is in them personally (ἐπί + accusative). But what of ἐν κυρίῳ 'in the Lord'? This appears to define the general area or context within which the confidence is expressed. Hence, it would seem to be a New Testament equivalent of our modern phrase "as a Christian." A particularly helpful example is Rom. 14:14, "I am convinced, in the Lord Jesus, that nothing is inherently unclean." This does not express an act of faith in the Lord Jesus (who is not described as doing anything) but an expression of Christian (as opposed to Jewish) conviction. Gal. 5:10 is very similar to the present verse (with εἰς ὑμᾶς for ἐφ' ὑμᾶς 'with respect to you'). Phil. 2:24, however, could be interpreted in such a way that the ἐν κυρίῳ 'in the Lord' is understood as expressing the one in whom the confidence is placed: "I am confident in the Lord that I myself will soon come to you."

However, since in 2 Thess. 3:4 there is ἐφ' ὑμᾶς 'with respect to you' as well as ἐν κυρίῳ 'in the Lord', and since the matter of confidence concerns the Thessalonians themselves, ἐν κυρίῳ is taken to be equivalent to "as Christians," and this finds expression in 3:4b as a reason proposition "*because you believe* in *our(inc)* Lord *Jesus*."

3:4c–d that you are obeying what we(exc) have commanded *you* and that you will obey what we(exc) are commanding *you in this letter*. These two propositions separate out what is compressed in the Greek. Although, in the Greek, reference is made to "you are doing" and "you will be doing," "what we command" is only expressed once and in the present tense. But, clearly, the present tense ποιεῖτε 'you are doing' presupposes that they had previously been instructed, and were now carrying out those instructions. (This would refer to the oral instructions given while Paul and his colleagues were in Thessalonica, and to those contained in 1 Thessalonians.)

The future form ποιήσετε 'you will be doing' is not so straightforward either. It could refer to the commands he had already issued in the letter (2:15; 3:1), or to those he was about to give them (3:6–15). Hence, in the display, the neutral "we are commanding you" is used, rather than the more precise "we have just commanded" and "we are about to command."

3:5a *We(exc) pray that our(inc)* **Lord Jesus would cause that you continue** *knowing* **that God loves** *you.* As in 2:15-16, the optative mood of the verb κατευθύνω 'direct' is considered to be a surface representation of the deep structure "we(exc) pray that."

3:5b-c *And we(exc) pray* **that** *our(inc)* **Lord Jesus will cause you to continue** *being* **steadfast like** *he,* **the Christ,** *was steadfast.* There are several exegetical matters common to these propositions, so they are discussed together.

The Greek uses figurative language for what the Lord is asked to do—κατευθύναι ὑμῶν τὰς καρδίας εἰς... 'direct your hearts into'. What is the nonfigurative equivalent? The verb translated "direct" (or "guide") is κατευθύνω and is only used in two other places in the New Testament (Luke 1:79, where Zechariah says that John the Baptist (or the coming Messiah) "will direct our feet into the path of peace," which would appear to mean either "show us how we may have peace" or "cause us to have peace"; and 1 Thess. 3:11, where it is used in a similar prayer "direct our way to you," which seems to mean "cause that we may be able to go to you," i.e., revisit the Thessalonians). Hence, the nonfigurative meaning is something like "cause someone to achieve a certain goal," and that would fit well here, especially collocated with εἰς 'into, towards', which is commonly associated with goals.

But why ὑμῶν τὰς καρδίας 'your hearts' rather than just ὑμᾶς 'you'? Perhaps because it is not physical movement that is involved in reaching these particular goals, but rather the inner life of the will and spiritual experience.

Following εἰς 'into' are two genitive constructions—τὴν ἀγάπην τοῦ θεοῦ 'the love of God' and τὴν ὑπομονὴν τοῦ Χριστοῦ 'the steadfastness of Christ'. In trying to decide how these should be understood, the following factors need weighing:

1. A number of commentators state that Paul uses the phrase "the love of God" only in the sense of God's love for men, not the reverse. This observation would appear to be correct, allowing for the fact that there will always be differences of opinion on individual verses. It also appears to be valid whether it is the Father, the Son (Rom. 8:35, 2 Cor. 5:14, Eph. 3:19), or the Spirit (Rom. 15:30) who is referred to. Verbal forms of ἀγαπάω 'to love' are used for the divine love for men, man's love for God, and love between Christians.

2. Since the whole clause is constructed in an obviously parallel way, both genitives are more likely to be interpreted in a parallel manner.

3. In the light of 1 and 2, "the steadfastness of Christ" (a unique phrase in the New Testament) could mean either "the steadfastness which Christ himself showed" or "the steadfastness which Christ gives to you." Either would make good sense here.

4. Why is Paul praying this particular prayer here? As has been pointed out in discussing 3:2-3 above, these verses probably presuppose a background of persecution—3:2 unambiguously does so, and 3:3 can easily be understood in that way also. And the word in this verse translated by "steadfastness" (ὑπομονή) is almost invariably associated with persecution in the New Testament (as was the case in 1:4). For the Thessalonians to experience ever more fully God's love for them, and to be steadfast, would certainly be appropriate prayers to pray in a general context of persecution.

If the interpretation of "the steadfastness of Christ" as "Christ causes you to be steadfast" is preferred, then this would simply mean omitting proposition 3:5c.

BOUNDARIES AND COHERENCE

The boundary between 3:2 and 3 has been discussed in connection with the preceding paragraph, and 3:5 coincides with the end of the section. It is the internal structure of 3:3-5 that is problematical.

It is far from clear how many semantic units there are. Each of the following approaches is possible:

1. There is one unit, consisting of 3:3-5.
2. There are two units, consisting of 3:3-4 and 3:5.
3. There are three units, each consisting of a verse.

There are no convincing arguments for any of these approaches. Each verse is introduced by δέ, so that would favor suggestion 3; 3:3 and 4 are statements, whereas 3:5 is a prayer, so that would favor suggestion 2; each verse refers to the Lord and "you(pl)," which would favor suggestion 1. In addition, a sort of "sandwich" arrangement can be observed if the patterns of reference to the participants are considered:

    A the Lord...you(pl) (3:3)
        B we(exc)...you(pl) (3:4)
    A' the Lord...you(pl) (3:5)

This tends to support the idea of a single unit also. The single unit view is followed in this analysis.

PROMINENCE AND THEME

This unit consists of three minimal paragraphs, each represented by a sentence in the Greek. Is any one of these three paragraphs more prominent semantically than the others, or are they equally prominent? The first paragraph is considered to be more prominent than the other two, but this is not, however, a straightforward or clearcut decision; the following are the factors that have led to it.

Since "the Lord" is a lexical motif in this section (as well as in the epistle as a whole), those propositions in which "the Lord" is the agent are considered to be more prominent than those in which this is not the case. This means that 3:3 and 5 are considered to be more prominent than 3:4.

But what is the relative prominence of 3:3 and 5? Verse 3:3 is a statement, and 3:5 is a prayer. Verses 2:16 and 17, which constitute a similar prayer using the optative mood, were analyzed as being the means of the nucleus proposition in the preceding section; the same suggestion is made here. The Lord will strengthen and protect them in answer to the prayers of Paul and his associates.

This makes 3:3 the nucleus of this paragraph. But that still leaves the question of the most prominent proposition(s) in 3:3 itself. Grammatically, the opening clause is the main one, being followed by a relative clause. Semantically, the proposition "the Lord is trustworthy" is a generic assertion and 3:3a and b express two specific conclusions drawn from it, as to how he will demonstrate his faithfulness to the Thessalonian believers in their particular circumstances. Hence, the conjoined propositions (3:3b and c) are regarded as constituting the thematic material of 3:3–5.

DIVISION CONSTITUENT 3:6–16a (Section: Nucleus₂ of the Body)

THEME: We(exc) command you to disassociate yourselves from every brother who refuses to work.	
RELATIONAL STRUCTURE	CONTENTS
NUCLEUS	3:6–11 We(exc) command you to disassociate yourselves from every brother who refuses to work.
— conjoined —	3:12 We(exc) command those brothers who are not working to support themselves by settling down and working.
— conjoined —	3:13 You others, do not stop doing what is right because you are discouraged.
— conjoined —	3:14–15 Publicly identify any brother who does not obey what we(exc) have written in this letter and do not associate with him.
— conjoined —	3:16a We(exc) pray that our(inc) Lord Jesus himself will give peace to you always and in every situation.

BOUNDARIES AND COHERENCE

Verse 3:6 is clearly marked as unit-initial by the vocative ἀδελφοί 'brothers', a new first person plural performative παραγγέλλομεν 'we command', and the conjunction δέ. But where does this section end? There are two possibilities: one is that it ends with 3:15, the other is that it ends with 3:16, more precisely, with 3:16a. In either case, the final verse is the end of the body of the letter, the remaining verses being the conclusion to the epistle as a whole. Thus, the question is: Where does the body of the epistle end?

In favor of 3:15 are the following sandwiching devices:

1. There is a second person plural present tense command both in 3:6 and in 3:14–15.
2. Verse 3:6 commands the church in Thessalonica to "disassociate" (στέλλεσθαι) itself from any believers who are not working for their living, and 3:14 has a similar command (μὴ συναναμίγνυσθαι 'not associate with').
3. Verse 3:6 refers to the teaching (παράδοσις) which Paul and his colleagues had passed on to the Thessalonians, and 3:14 refers to the teaching (λόγος) of this letter itself.

In favor of adding 3:16 are:

1. The use of δέ in 3:16. This is significant, since δέ does not occur in epistle endings.
2. The pattern of prayers ending sections in this epistle. If 3:16 is not included in this section, then it would be the only section without a terminal prayer. In addition, the form of the prayer, opening as it does with αὐτὸς δὲ ὁ κύριος '(may) the Lord himself', is exactly the same as in 2:16, and very similar to 3:5 (which lacks the emphatic αὐτός 'himself'); and all three use the (rare) optative mood.

Hence, the analysis preferred in the display is to treat 3:16 as a prayer, closing the final section of the body, and hence, the body itself. (For the choice of 3:16a, rather than all of 3:16, see the discussion on section constituent 3:16a.)

Coherence is shown in this section by repeated references to:

1. You(pl)—every verse except 3:12.
2. We(exc)—every verse except 3:13, 15, and 16.
3. The cluster of related concepts (in this context) of "disorderly" (ἀτάκτως in 3:6 and 11; ἀτακτέω in 3:7), "working" (ἐργάζομαι in 3:8, 10, 11, 12), "eating" (ἐσθίω in 3:8, 10, 12).
4. The threefold use of παραγγέλλω 'to command' in 3:6, 10, and 12.
5. The references to the Lord (κύριος in 3:6, 12, 16).

PROMINENCE AND THEME

This section consists of a series of semantic units whose main proposition is a command, apart from the closing prayer in 3:16. How is it to be decided which command, if any, is more prominent than the others? The following are the factors taken into consideration:

1. Unit 3:12 is regarded as less prominent than the other commands as it is addressed to a minority group within the church, and the content is, in any case, implied by the command developed in 3:6–11.
2. Unit 3:13 is regarded as less prominent than 3:6–11 and 3:14–15 as it is undeveloped, and is not closely related to the rest of the section.
3. Unit 3:14–15 is more problematical. It seems best to regard it as supplementary to the command in 3:6. In 3:6 the believers are commanded to withdraw themselves from any fellow believers who are not working, and these same nonworkers are commanded in 3:12 to work for their living. In 3:14–15, the possible situation is envisaged in which one or more of the nonworkers might disobey the command in 3:12, and instructions are given to the congregation as to what to do in these circumstances. Hence, 3:14–15 is analyzed as less prominent in that it handles a special case within the more general one.

If these arguments are correct, then 3:6–11 would be the most prominent constituent of this section. This conclusion is probably supported by the fact that it is the only constituent of this section which is introduced by both a performative and a vocative. (Verse 3:12 has a performative, but no vocative; 3:13 has a vocative, but no performative; and 3:14–15 has neither.) Also, 3:6–11 is the most developed of the constituents, with grounds expressed in detail; in fact, none of the other commands is supported by a grounds constituent.

The theme, then, of section 3:6–16a is the same as the theme of the nucleus paragraph (3:6–11).

SECTION CONSTITUENT 3: 6–11 (Paragraph: Nucleus of 3:6–16a)

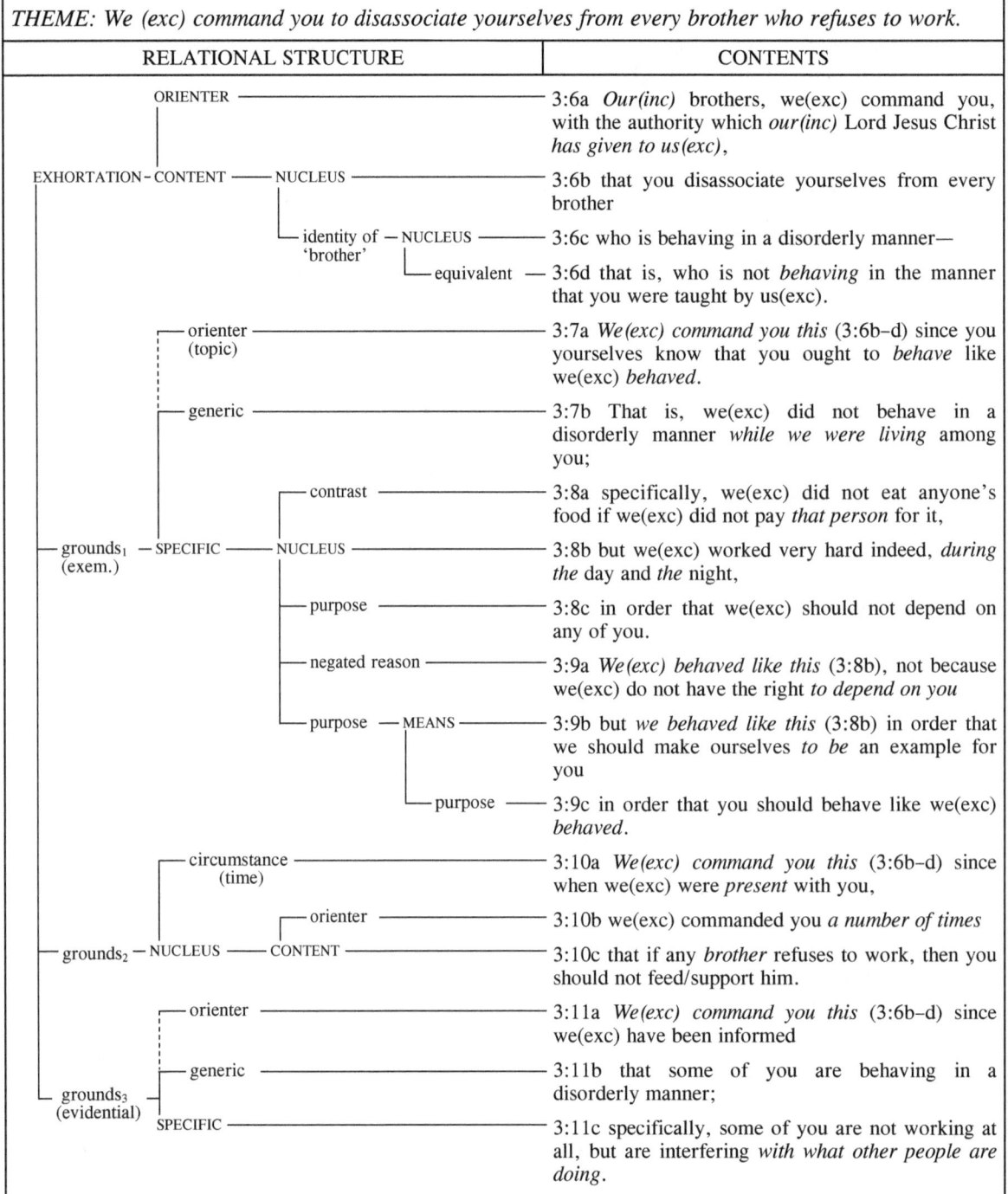

NOTES

3:6a *Our(inc)* brothers, we(exc) command you, with the authority which *our(inc)* Lord Jesus Christ *has given to us(exc)*, It is very widely agreed that ἐν ὀνόματι τοῦ... 'in the name of...' is semantically equivalent to "with the authority of." The problem of the idle brothers was not a minor one—it was serious enough for Paul to use the verb παραγγέλλω 'to command', and to refer explicitly to the divine authority behind what was said.

3:6b that you disassociate yourselves from every brother Quite a few different translations are given for the verb στέλλεσθαι, such as to "shun," "avoid," "withdraw from," "hold aloof from," and 'keep away from." The commentaries stress that it is not excommunication that is referred to, i.e., official expulsion from the local church, but social ostracism to show the disapproval of the majority for the minority who were misbehaving in this way. "Disassociate" is chosen for the display because it carries the components of (a) previously associating with these brothers, but now not doing so; and (b) showing disapproval, in this way, of their conduct.

3:6c who is behaving in a disorderly manner— There is some question as to whether the adverb ἀτάκτως should be translated by "disorderly" or by "idly." Elsewhere in Greek writings, it is used of soldiers in disarray, of students playing truant, of citizens disregarding civil regulations. It is clear from the rest of this paragraph that the particular form of disorderliness that Paul has in mind is that of not working for one's living, but this gave rise to other evils such as "sponging" on others and being "busybodies." Hence, it seems preferable to keep the more generic sense of "disorderly" rather than replace it by "idly" since a group of associated evils is in mind. Paul's use of "disorderly" rather than simply "idly" probably shows that he was regarding this voluntary idleness seriously. It was not just a matter of being lazy; it was a rejection of the principle, established at creation, that man should work.

3:6d that is, who is not *behaving* **in the manner that you were taught by us(exc).** Literally translated, the clause underlying this proposition is "not (walking) in accordance with the teaching which they/you received from us." There are two minor comments:

1. The word translated "teaching" is παράδοσις which means "the teachings committed to us," i.e., the word itself carries the component that Paul and his colleagues did not originate the teachings, but were simply transmitting what the Lord had committed to them. (It has already been used in 2:15.)
2. The "they/you" choice (παρελάβοσαν/-ον 'they received' versus παρελάβετε 'you(pl) received') reflects part of the variety of textual choices here.

The "they" refers back to "every brother" in 3:6b, and is included in the "you" alternative, which refers to all the believers at Thessalonica. It is better, therefore, to use the more inclusive "you" since, in languages with an exclusive component to pronouns, "they" would imply "not the rest of you," which is obviously not the case—all heard the teaching.

3:7a *We(exc) command you this* (3:6b–d) since you yourselves know that you ought to *behave like we(exc) behaved*. This proposition introduces the topic of the first grounds propositional cluster (3:7–9), which is how the Thessalonian believers should live like Paul and his colleagues had lived. Paul is going to remind them of what they already knew from his teaching and the example of himself, Silas, and Timothy—namely, that they had an obligation, as believers, to support themselves by working for their living. The topic is their behavior; the comment is a specific manner of behaving.

3:7b That is, we(exc) did not behave in a disorderly manner *while we were living* **among you;** This is a general and negative statement of the manner, using the same generic concept "disorderly" as was used in 3:6c.

3:8a specifically, we(exc) did not eat anyone's food if we(exc) did not pay *that person* **for it,** This proposition gives a specific statement of what sort of "disorderliness" Paul had in mind, namely, not working for one's own living. "We did not eat anyone's food" does not mean Paul and his colleagues refused offers of hospitality, but rather that they supported themselves by paying their own way. Whether they lived in a fellow believer's home, or rented somewhere for themselves, they paid for it, and for their food.

3:8b but we(exc) worked very hard indeed, *during the* **day and** *the* **night** "Very hard" represents a doublet in the Greek, the second word of which (μόχθος) is found collocated only with the first word (κόπος) in the New Testament; the other instances are in 2 Cor. 11:27 and 1 Thess. 2:9. It is an intensive doublet, underlining how hard they had worked.

Νυκτὸς καὶ ἡμέρας 'night and day', represented in the display in the more common English order, "day and night," is descriptive of long hours, both during the day and during the night, but not twenty-four hours continuously. The work is the manual work of earning their living. Obviously, Paul and the others must have given as much time as they could to preaching and teaching (cf. 1 Thess. 2:9), as well as taking some time for eating and sleeping.

3:8c in order that we(exc) should not depend on any of you. "Depend on any of you" pertains to board and room. Although Paul's primary purpose in supporting himself was to set the Thessalonians an example to follow (3:9c), a secondary purpose was to avoid being a financial burden on any of the believers.

3:9a-c *We(exc) behaved like this* **(3:8b), not because we(exc) did not have the right** *to depend on you* **but** *we behaved like this* **(3:8b) in order that we should make ourselves** *to be* **an example for you in order that you should behave like we(exc)** *behaved*. The first part of 3:9a is a repeat, in the display, not the Greek, of 3:8b to make the flow of the argument clearer. It is repeated again in 3:9b for the same reasons.

Ἐξουσία 'right' is only mentioned in passing here—Paul refers to the right of the spiritual worker to be supported by those who were benefiting from his ministry. Paul and his colleagues had waived this right in Thessalonica so as to be an example of hard work to the Thessalonians (see 3:9c).

3:10a-b *We(exc) command you this* **(3:6b-d) since when we(exc) were** *present* **with you, we(exc) commanded you** *a number of times* The phrase "a number of times" is used to represent the imperfect tense of the Greek verb παρηγγέλλομεν, which implies that Paul and his colleagues had spoken to the Thessalonian believers on a number of occasions about this particular matter of supporting themselves.

3:10c that if any *brother* **refuses to work, then you should not feed/support him.** The content of the command (in 3:10b) is prominent, as is shown in the Greek by the deictic τοῦτο 'this' preceding the verb and referring forward to the content of the verb.

The Greek τις 'any person' is very general. Paul, however, is not issuing instructions for the community in general, but for the believers, so τις is understood to mean here "any brother." An alternative would be "any of you," but the former is better in the light of the general way the principle in 3:10c is expressed.

The force of the Greek οὐ θέλει is either "does not want" or "refuses." The implication is that such a brother could work (i.e., he was not ill, disabled, old, etc.) but, for whatever reasons, he would not do so, and so became dependent on the generosity of the Christian community.

The Greek underlying the last part of this proposition is μηδὲ ἐσθιέτω 'then let him not be eating'. In the context, this means that the Christian congregation should not be responsible for feeding any Christian brother who did not earn his living, when he could have done so. As is generally the case, a third person imperative is one form in which a command can be expressed. Here, the command is addressed to the Thessalonian church.

3:11 Most commentators attach this verse to 3:10, as an explanation or grounds for Paul repeating this command. In the display, however, the conjunction γάρ 'for' is taken as signaling a third grounds for the command in 3:6, namely, the evidential grounds that the situation was already present in the church at Thessalonica, and so needed to be dealt with.

3:11a-b *We(exc) command you this* **(3:6b-d) since we(exc) have been informed that some of you are behaving in a disorderly manner;** The present tense is used in the Greek (ἀκούομεν 'we hear') and may mean that Paul and the others had received several reports about the idle members, or it may simply mean that they had heard. Again, "to hear" in this context means they had been informed, not necessarily orally, though that is quite likely. Hence, "we have been informed" conveys the sense well.

3:11c specifically, some of you are not working at all, but are interfering *with what other people are doing.* As all the commentators point out, the Greek for "working," ἐργαζομένους, and for "being busybodies," περιεργαζομένους, are very similar, and Paul was using a play on words to make his point. The latter word is used only here in the New Testament, but the corresponding adjective is used in 1 Tim. 5:13 (where the SSA of 1 Timothy translates it with "to meddle"). It has the meaning of engaging in useless or irrelevant activities, and hence, meddling or being involved in other people's affairs. It is generally thought that, since they were not occupied with earning their living, these idle brothers were going around "visiting" other believers, and generally being a nuisance as a result.

BOUNDARIES AND COHERENCE

The initial boundary is clearly marked, as it coincides with the section boundary (see discussion above). But there is a considerable difference of opinion over where this unit should end. Basically, there are three alternatives—to end with 3:10, with 3:11, or with 3:12.

The main reason put forward for breaking after 3:10 is that 3:11 refers explicitly to "some who are behaving in a disorderly manner," and 3:12 uses the anaphoric τοῖς τοιούτοις 'such people'. Hence, it is argued, 3:11 and 12 belong together. The principal objection to separating 3:11-12 from 3:6-10 is the occurrence of the conjunction γάρ 'for' initially in 3:11, as this conjunction always follows what it relates to, never precedes it. Hence, 3:11 is linked backwards, not forwards.

The case for ending this unit with 3:12 is a strong one. Firstly, 3:13 is marked by the occurrence of the vocative ἀδελφοί 'brothers'; the particle δέ (which is nearly always paragraph initial in this letter); and a new, semantically distinct imperative. So there is good evidence for a boundary at the end of 3:12. In addition, it is pointed out that there is a sandwich structure, in that the performative παραγγέλλομεν 'we command', backed by the authority of the Lord Jesus Christ, occurs in 3:6 and 12.

The question, therefore, comes down to this: Are there sufficiently good reasons for making a boundary at the end of 3:11? The following reasons are proposed:

1. Verse 3:12 has a new group of addressees indicated by a forefronted noun phrase, so that Paul is no longer addressing the total congregation as in 3: 6-11.
2. Verse 3:12 has the conjunction δέ, which strengthens the case for a new paragraph.
3. Logically, 3:11 completes the sequence of thought, so that 3:12 starts over again.
4. Verse 3:12 is better considered to be another start, parallel to 3:6, rather than the close of a sandwich structure, since it is a new command, i.e., the content is different from that of 3:6.

It is suggested, therefore, that 3:12 is a separate constituent of section 3:6-16a. It is obviously similar to 3:6-11 in several ways, but is nevertheless a distinct unit.

Verses 3:6-11 are clearly marked so far as coherence is concerned:

1. We(exc) is referred to in every verse.
2. You(pl) is also referred to in every verse.
3. Disorderly behavior is referred to in 3:6 (ἀτάκτως περιπατοῦντος 'behaving in a disorderly manner'), 3:7 ((οὐκ) ἠτακτήσαμεν 'we did (not) behave in a disorderly manner'), and 3:11 (περιπατοῦντας ἀτάκτως 'behaving in a disorderly manner').
4. The concepts opposed to "disorderly behavior" are "working" and "eating" and these are referred to in 3:8, 10, and 11.
5. The paragraph is relationally coherent in that it consists of a command (3:6), followed by three grounds, each introduced by γάρ 'for' (3:7, 10, 11).

PROMINENCE AND THEME

As stated in point 5 above, this paragraph consists of an exhortation (3:6) followed by three different grounds supporting it, each introduced by γάρ 'for'. None of these grounds is marked as prominent, so the opening exhortation is the most prominent information.

However, there are two further matters to be considered before the final form of the theme can be established.

The command is introduced by the performative παραγγέλλομεν 'we command', which is regarded as part of the theme statement, since it is a hortatory performative in a hortatory section. However, the circumstantial phrase "with the authority...given to us" is omitted from the theme statement, since it is not a performative, but simply modifies it adverbially.

The command refers to "every brother who is behaving in a disorderly manner." However, it is clear from the grounds attached to the command that the identificational relative clause is generic, and that the particular form of disorderliness that had arisen in Thessalonica was that of not working for one's living. This is another case where a single specific is considered to be more prominent than the generic to which it is related. Hence, the identifying proposition of 3:6 is replaced by "who refuses to work," the form used in 3:10c. The problem was not simply that some of the Christians were not working for their living, but that they were not willing to do so. Hence, the stronger description is used in the theme statement. (When the paragraph 3:14-15 is also considered, it would appear that "refuses to work" is after being informed of Paul's command in 3:12 that they should support themselves. Hence, the refusal is a refusal to obey the authoritative command of the apostle.)

SECTION CONSTITUENT 3:12 (Propositional Cluster: Conjoined to 3:6–11)

THEME: We(exc) command those brothers who are not working to support themselves by settling down and working.

RELATIONAL STRUCTURE	CONTENTS
ORIENTER — NUCLEUS₁	3:12a We(exc) command those brothers who are not working
nucleus₂	3:12b and we(exc) urge *them*,
grounds	3:12c *since we(exc) and they believe* in *our(inc)* Lord Jesus Christ,
CONTENT — RESULT	3:12d that they support themselves
MEANS	3:12e by their *settling down and working.

NOTES

3:12a–b We(exc) command those brothers who are not working and we(exc) urge *them*, The Greek for 3:12a is τοῖς τοιούτοις παραγγέλλομεν 'to the such we command', "the such" being the nonworkers, referred to throughout the previous paragraph. Since 3:12 is analyzed as a unit distinct from 3:6–11, the back reference is replaced by the identifying proposition "the brothers who are not working."

3:12c *since we(exc) and they believe* in *our(inc)* Lord Jesus Christ, There is a choice of text here, modern versions following ἐν κυρίῳ Ἰησοῦ Χριστῷ 'in (the) Lord Jesus Christ, and the older versions following διὰ τοῦ κυρίου ἡμῶν Ἰησοῦ Χριστοῦ 'by/through (our) Lord Jesus Christ. The UBS third edition of the Greek New Testament does not refer to this variant, nor does the Textual Commentary, so I assume it is rejected as poorly supported. However, the Majority Text has διά 'by/through'. (See the following discussion for any possible difference in meaning.)

It is not easy to decide what either prepositional phrase could mean here. If ἐν 'in' is preferred, it seems likely that Paul is making his appeal to the erring brothers on the grounds that he who exhorts, and they who are being exhorted, are all believers in Christ, united by that common bond. If διά 'by/through' is chosen, it seems likely that more stress is being placed on the authority of the Lord (cf. 1 Thess. 4:2, where the same preposition is used). In that case, it would be a stylistic variant of the phrase "in the name of our Lord Jesus Christ" in 3:6; see 3:6a for the way it is handled there. It is also possible that "in the Lord Jesus Christ" could refer to his authority, it being regarded as an abbreviation of "in the name of" in 3:6. The main argument against this view here is that Paul has "softened" the direct "we command" by adding his more usual "we urge/exhort" to it, so it seems a little unlikely that he would then stress his authority.

3:12d that they support themselves Τὸν ἑαυτῶν ἄρτον ἐσθίωσιν 'eat their own food' is understood as meaning "provide for themselves," not depending on others to provide their food.

3:12e by their *settling down and working. The clause representing the means proposition is placed before the main clause in the Greek, so is analyzed as having marked prominence, giving it equal semantic rank with the main proposition.

There is some discussion as to the exact meaning of the phrase μετὰ ἡσυχίας 'with calmness' here. In the context, it is very likely that it expresses the opposite of that excited state of mind that (it is assumed) had led some of the Thessalonian believers to give up their work, and go around "meddling" with other believers. They were to calm down, and settle down (NIV) to some good steady work. The phrase is highlighted in the Greek by being initial in the content of the exhortation, and this is shown in the display by using the verb "to settle down" rather than an adverb. "To settle down" is asterisked because it is not being used in its primary sense of "take up residence somewhere," but the secondary sense of ceasing to be agitated and returning to normal behavior.

BOUNDARIES AND COHERENCE

The boundaries of this unit have already been discussed in connection with paragraph 3:6–11 (above).

In such a short unit there is always less evidence for coherence, but note:

1. References to "those who are not working" in each of the four clauses.
2. The use of the present tense throughout.
3. The close-knit relational "chain" linking the clauses.
4. Grammatically, the fact that it is a single sentence.

PROMINENCE AND THEME

Like the unit which precedes it, this semantic unit consists of a (hortatory) performative orienter with its content, so both are regarded as thematic since the genre is hortatory. But note the following points:

1. There are actually two performatives παραγγέλλομεν 'we command' and παρακαλοῦμεν 'we urge' linked by καί 'and'. Since "we command" parallels the performative in 3:6 above, and is the first of the two performatives, it is considered to be the more prominent of the two.
2. Since the clause representing the means proposition precedes the main clause, it is regarded as having marked prominence, and so is thematic.
3. The adverbial phrase μετὰ ἡσυχίας 'with calmness' is highlighted within the means proposition, so is also regarded as thematic. Since English is being used as the language of the display, this prominence is most readily shown by expressing the means proposition in a conjoined form "by settling down and working," where "by settling down" represents "with calmness."

SECTION CONSTITUENT 3:13 (Propositional Cluster: Conjoined to 3:6–11)

THEME: *You others, do not stop doing what is right because you are discouraged.*	
RELATIONAL STRUCTURE	CONTENTS
NUCLEUS ———————	3:13 You *others*, *our(inc)* brothers, do not stop doing what is right because you are discouraged.

NOTES

3:13 You *others*, *our(inc)* brothers, do not stop doing what is right because you are discouraged. The forefronted ὑμεῖς 'you(pl)' has been explained above as indicating a return to the original addressees, i.e., those in 3:6–11, after a new group has been addressed in 3:12. "You (others)" has been used in the display to indicate this, where "others" means strictly "you who are not idle brothers."

The command ἐγκακήσητε 'do not give up' is in the aorist aspect, and so probably carries the implication that they were not giving up at the time of writing, but that Paul is warning them against that danger. While "to give up" or "be weary in" are the usual English translations, the Greek verb is regarded as representing a complex concept "to stop (doing something) because you are discouraged or weary of doing it," which is "unraveled" in the display.

It is possible that καλοποιοῦντες 'doing good' could mean "treating your erring brothers properly," but a more generic sense is preferred here. Undoubtedly, patience towards their troublesome, idle brothers was included, as well as not following their error; but Paul may have also had in mind the pressure of the persecutions referred to in chapter 1, and the temptation to give up as a result, and so to avoid the suffering. It is, in effect, a call to steadfastness, to steady persistence in Christian behavior, in spite of the problems they faced.

BOUNDARIES AND COHERENCE

The initial boundary of this unit is clearly marked by the occurrence of the vocative ἀδελφοί 'brothers', and the conjunction δέ. In addition, there is a forefronted ὑμεῖς 'you(pl)', signaling that

Paul is again addressing the majority of the congregation at Thessalonica, all those who were not included in the command in 3:12. Hence, there is a change of addressee.

More problematical is where this unit ends. Should 3:13 be treated as a unit on its own, a brief command to the majority, or should it be analyzed as the opening verse in a unit consisting of 3:13–15?

The principal argument in favor of regarding 3:13–15 as a single unit is the fact that it consists of a series of second person plural commands addressed to the majority of the congregation who had not given up working for their living. In support of this, the last word in 3:13, καλοποιοῦντες 'doing good', could be interpreted, in this context, as meaning "treating (the erring brothers) properly/well." In other words, 3:13 is seen as a command not to give up on the idle brothers, but to keep acting towards them as Christian brothers, even though these misguided brothers were not showing much obvious signs of improvement. This certainly makes good sense in the total context, and would be an acceptable interpretation.

However, the analysis of 3:13 as a separate unit is considered the better one. The arguments leading to this decision are the following:

1. Although it is true that 3:13, 14, and 15 all contain second person plural commands, the command in 3:13 is aorist, whereas those in 3:14 and 15 are present tense. Further, they deal with different matters—3:13, their behavior in general; 3:14 and 15, how they should treat any brother who disobeys the commands in the letter. Even if καλοποιοῦντες 'doing good' is interpreted as above, there is still a shift, but a lesser one, from the erring idle brothers in general, to any erring brother who persists in his misguided ways after hearing Paul's commands.
2. Verse 3:14 has the conjunction δέ, which strengthens the case for 3:13 being a separate unit.
3. The "if" of 3:14a is clearly related to 3:14b, and 3:15 also relates back to 3:14b. Hence, there is no obvious relation between 3:14–15 on the one hand and 3:13 on the other.
4. The forefronted τις 'anyone' in 3:14 announces a new topic, namely, "anyone who disobeys the command contained in this letter." Instructions are then given as to what to do concerning this type of person. This new topic is certainly related to the preceding topics, but is nevertheless distinct.

Hence, 3:13 is regarded as a brief, general exhortation to the majority of the congregation, following on the much longer, more specific one, in 3:6–11, and also preceding a more specific one in 3:14–15.

It is interesting to note that, in the Greek, apart from the two particles δέ 'and (next)' and μή 'not', every form carries a second person plural reference, overtly or implicitly.

PROMINENCE. AND THEME

There is skewing between the Greek form and the propositional analysis, in that in the Greek the reason proposition is represented by the main verb ἐγκακήσητε 'do not get discouraged', and the main proposition by the participle καλοποιοῦντες 'doing good'. This highlights the reason and makes it thematic. Hence, the theme statement is essentially the same as the unit itself. However, the vocative is not regarded as thematic and is omitted since it signals the pragmatics of the situation, rather than prominent information. The referential significance of the forefronted ὑμεῖς you(pl) is retained, so that it is clear, in the context of the section as a whole, who is being addressed.

SECTION CONSTITUENT 3:14–15 (Paragraph: Conjoined to 3:6–11)

THEME: Publicly identify any brother who does not obey what we(exc) have written in this letter and do not associate with him.

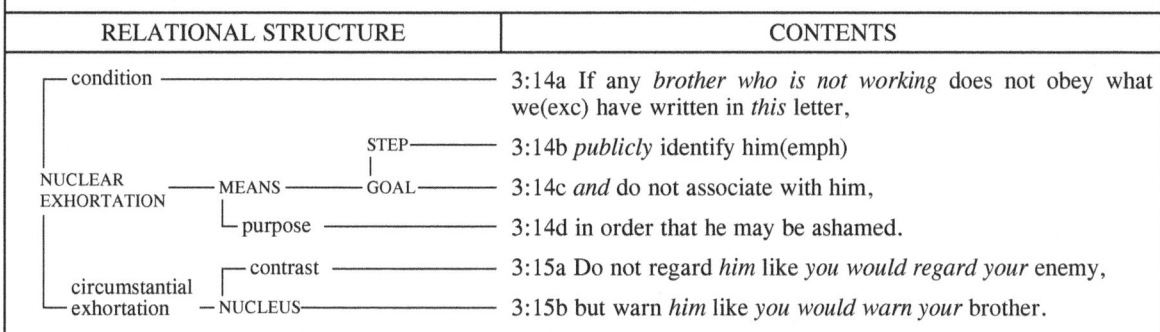

RELATIONAL STRUCTURE	CONTENTS
condition	3:14a If any *brother who is not working* does not obey what we(exc) have written in *this* letter,
NUCLEAR EXHORTATION — MEANS — STEP	3:14b *publicly* identify him(emph)
— GOAL	3:14c *and* do not associate with him,
— purpose	3:14d in order that he may be ashamed.
circumstantial exhortation — contrast	3:15a Do not regard *him* like *you would regard your* enemy,
— NUCLEUS	3:15b but warn *him* like *you would warn your* brother.

NOTES

3:14a If any *brother who is not working* does not obey what we(exc) have written in *this* letter, The Greek simply says τις 'any', but in the context it clearly means "any brother among you," and most commentators refer the disobedience back to the command in 3:12, so that "any" means "any brother who is not working," the same reference as in 3:12a.

3:14b *publicly* identify him(emph) How the "noting" was to be done is not specified, but could possibly affect the translation. Evidently, his name was to be known to the whole congregation, so that they could act unitedly, so it could well have been announced at some public meeting of the whole church. Hence, σημειοῦσθε 'note' is represented in the display by "publicly identify." The τοῦτον 'him' is emphatic.

3:14c–d *and* do not associate with him, in order that he may be ashamed. The textual and grammatical questions are discussed under prominence and theme. With either textual variant, it seems semantically necessary to regard 3:14c as a command, and the main command; any such disobedient brother was to be avoided. Again, it is not clear just exactly what this "avoiding" involved, since he was to be warned, and generally treated as a Christian brother. Hence, total ostracism would appear to be excluded. It seems reasonable to assume that the main command here is semantically the same as that in 3:6. This paragraph adds the details of public identification, and how he is to be regarded.

3:15a–b Do not regard *him* like *you would regard your* enemy, but warn *him* like *you would warn your* brother. The verb νουθετέω 'warn' carries the components of (a) a warm relationship between the parties concerned (such as parents and children, friends, brothers) and (b) that the one who is the object of the verb is in error of some sort, doctrinal or behavioral, or in danger of falling into error. Hence, "warn" is a suitable translation in English. However, the old English "admonish" represents the components of the Greek verb more accurately.

BOUNDARIES AND COHERENCE

The reasons for regarding 3:14 as the beginning of a new unit have been discussed in connection with the previous unit, and 3:15 is the last verse in this unit which is hortatory in genre, 3:16 being a prayer.

The coherence of this unit is shown in several ways:

1. Three present tense second person plural commands occur in the unit: σημειοῦσθε 'note', ἡγεῖσθε 'regard', and νουθετεῖτε 'warn'.
2. There are several references to "anyone who disobeys our message" (τις 'anyone' in 3:14a, τοῦτον 'this one' in 3:14b, αὐτῷ 'him' in 3:14c, ἐντραπῇ 'he be ashamed' in 3:14d, ἐχθρόν 'enemy' and ἀδελφόν 'brother' in 3:15).
3. Relationally, this unit consists of two sentences connected by καί 'and', showing that the same topic is still under consideration.

PROMINENCE AND THEME

This is a difficult paragraph from a prominence standpoint, as the formal signals and the relational structure are rather out of step with each other.

The first command is "note him," "him" being defined in the first half of the verse, and "note" being a finite verb in the imperative mood (σημειοῦσθε).

In most modern texts, this is followed by an infinitive, grammatically dependent on the command, but with the grammars uncertain as to whether to treat it as an infinitive of purpose, or as expressing a second (dependent) command. On the other hand, the Majority Text has a straightforward finite imperative. In either case, from *a relational* standpoint, it is hard to avoid the conclusion that the "noting" is a step or means to the end of "not associating" (μὴ συναναμίγνυσθαι/ε) with any such brother, and that therefore it is the "not associating" that is most important, not the "noting." Hence, "not associating" is taken as the nucleus proposition, but the "noting" as a prominent step, of equal rank, since it is a finite imperative, whereas, following the modern texts, the nucleus proposition is in the form of an infinitive. It is also in a tight grammatical relationship with the nucleus clause. If the Majority Text is followed, so that the nucleus proposition is represented by a finite imperative verb, then the step proposition, 3:14b, would not be regarded as prominent and thematic.

There are two further commands in 3:15, both finite. These are in contrast with each other, so the command "warn him as a brother" is the more prominent of the two, as it is the positive side of the contrast. But how does it relate to the nucleus command in 3:14c? It seems best to analyze 3:15 as giving two contrasting circumstances associated with the main command, that is to say, two other events, one negative and one positive, that were to go on simultaneously with the main event. Verse 3:15 is therefore analyzed as supporting the main command, and hence not thematic. The fact that 3:15 is expressed in the form of two commands reflects the fact the genre is hortatory, rather than the fact that 3:15 is prominent.

Hence, the theme statement is considered to consist of a prominent step as well as the nucleus proposition itself.

SECTION CONSTITUENT 3:16a (Propositional Cluster: Conjoined to 3:6–11)

THEME: We(exc) pray that our(inc) Lord Jesus himself will give peace to you always and in every situation.	
RELATIONAL STRUCTURE	CONTENTS
NUCLEUS ——————————	3:16a *We(exc) pray that our(inc)* Lord *Jesus* himself, who gives *peace *to his people*, will give *peace to you always and in every situation.

NOTES

3:16a *We(exc) pray that our(inc)* Lord *Jesus* himself, who gives *peace *to his people*, will give *peace to you always and in every situation. The description proposition "who *gives* *peace *to his people*" represents the interpretation of a genitive construction ὁ κύριος τῆς εἰρήνης 'the Lord of peace'. This use of the genitive construction to signal the source or origin of something is widely used in the New Testament epistles, usually with God—"God of hope," "God of comfort," etc.

In this general sort of prayer "peace" is to be understood in its general Christian sense of "spiritual wellbeing." There is no reference to dissensions in the Thessalonian church, so it should not be understood in its more specific sense of harmony between factious elements. Some commentators say that it is almost equivalent to "salvation" here, or, more strictly, all the blessings that accompany salvation.

The biblical collocation of "give peace" has been kept, but the acceptability of such a collocation in other languages will depend very much on how "peace" is expressed lexically in them.

Some commentators take the final phrase ἐν παντὶ τρόπῳ to mean "in every way" but, collocationally, "in every situation/circumstance" handles this reference to variety better. The textual variant ἐν παντὶ τόπῳ 'in every place' is not nearly so well supported in the MSS and probably arose as a natural mistake from familiarity with it as a more commonly used phrase (1 Cor. 1:2; 2 Cor. 2:14; 1 Thess. 1:8; 1 Tim. 2:8). Contextually, also, "in every circumstance" is preferable to "in every place," since there is nothing in the immediate or more remote context to suggest that the Thessalonians were moving about (as in the list of references given above).

BOUNDARIES AND COHERENCE

The initial boundary of this unit is clearly indicated by the forefronted subject, the occurrence of δέ, and the change of subgenre from commands to prayer, shown by the switch from the imperative to the optative mood.

But where does it end? There are various possibilities, but this discussion will concentrate on one particular—and crucial—question: Does 3:16 initiate the end of the epistle as a whole, or is it the end of the body, with 3:17–18 constituting the end of the epistle? The first of these alternatives is very widely accepted, but some versions, such as the RSV, NEB, the Living Bible, Weymouth, and Goodspeed attach 3:16 to the body of the letter, and separate off 3:17–18 as the closing part of the epistle.

Faced with this decision, I made a study of the pattern of the endings of Paul's letters. The textual problems connected with Romans made it difficult to use it as evidence, so there were twelve endings available for study. It is possible to formulate the following overall pattern for the material that Paul uses to close an epistle, i.e., that follows the end of the body of the letter. There are six possible items, occurring in the following order:

1. A statement that someone will bring news about himself.
2. Greetings and final instructions.
3. A brief verbless prayer.
4. Paul's personal greeting.
5. A remark.
6. A final "grace be with you" prayer.

In 1 Corinthians, uniquely, a second (verbless) prayer follows the "grace" at the very end, but in all the other epistles, the "grace" is the actual end.

The greetings are usually from those present with Paul to individuals who will hear the letter, together with a general command to greet those receiving the letter, and they may occur in either order. The brief prayer is always verbless. Paul's personal greeting is in the identical form Ὁ ἀσπασμὸς τῇ ἐμῇ χειρὶ Παύλου 'the greeting of

Paul, by my own hand'. The final "grace" always starts with ἡ χάρις 'grace'.

No one letter has all six places filled, but Col. 4:7–18 exemplifies all of them except the verbless prayer. The other letters have four or less of the places filled.

One important observation arising in connection with this analysis is that all sentences found in the epistle endings, with two exceptions, lack conjunction. The exceptions are δέ in Eph. 6:21, in which Paul says news of him will be brought by Tychicus; and the final instructions in Col. 4:16–17, which are linked by καί 'and'. This immediately raises questions about the status of 3:16 in this epistle, as it has the sentence conjunction δέ. The conclusion I would draw is that, as a number of versions also indicate, it is to be considered the end of the body rather than of the epistle. This conclusion is confirmed by the recurrent pattern in 2 Thessalonians of a prayer terminating a section. If 3:16 is assigned to the epistle ending, only this section, from 3:6–15, would lack such a terminal prayer.

However, a closer look at 3:16 shows that it contains two separate prayers—one introduced by δέ and with a finite verb; and the other with no conjunction and no verb. Although this verse is generally treated as a unit, it fits in best with the pattern of the endings of Paul's other letters if the verbless prayer, without conjunction and verb, is treated as belonging to the epistle ending, and not the body ending. It is, in fact, very similar to the verbless prayer in 2 Tim. 4:22a which reads, "The Lord (be) with your(sg) spirit," the prayer here being, "The Lord (be) with you all."

Hence, 3:16a is regarded as the end of the body of the letter. Verse 3:16b opens the ending of the epistle itself, as Paul includes no greetings from or to others in this letter, nor any final instructions. The verbless prayer of 3:16b is followed by Paul's personal greeting in 3:17 and the "grace" in 3:18. (I realize that this analytical decision is awkward for a translator, as it splits 3:16 between two separate paragraphs making numbering difficult. If this is a problem, all of 3:16 is best treated as the body-final paragraph.)

PROMINENCE AND THEME

All that has been omitted from this propositional cluster for the theme statement is the description proposition "who *gives* *peace *to his people*." It is debatable, however, whether the two adverbial modifiers "all the time" and "in every situation" should be included in a theme statement or not, but in the present state of knowledge they are included.

EPISTLE CONSTITUENT 3:16b–18 (Paragraph: closing of the Epistle)

THEME: In closing, we(exc) pray that our(inc) Lord Jesus will continue to bless you all. I, Paul, am greeting you and I am writing this myself in order that you may know that I, Paul, have sent this letter.

RELATIONAL STRUCTURE	CONTENTS
NUCLEUS₁	3:16b *We(exc)/I pray that* our(inc) Lord *Jesus will continue to be present* with you all.
NUCLEUS₂ — NUCLEUS₁	3:17a I, Paul, am greeting *you*
NUCLEUS₂ — NUCLEUS	3:17b *and* I am writing *this* (3:17–18) myself
comparison	3:17c *as I do* in all my letters
purpose	3:17d *in order that* you may know *that I, Paul, have sent this letter.*
comment	3:17e This is the way I write.
NUCLEUS₃	3:18 *We(exc)/I pray that* our(inc) Lord Jesus Christ *will continue to* act graciously to you all.

NOTES

3:16b *We(exc)/I pray that* our(inc) Lord *Jesus will continue to be present* with you all. The Greek simply says ὁ κύριος μετὰ πάντων ὑμῶν 'the Lord with all you'. It is widely agreed that, because of the context, this is a prayer, not a statement, and that "the Lord" is the Lord Jesus, as throughout the prayers in this letter, and as explicitly stated below in 3:18. The implied verb is taken to be "to be present" as is indicated by the use of the preposition μετά 'with'. It also seems reasonable to assume that Paul and his colleagues were not praying that the Lord Jesus would now start to be present with the Thessalonian believers, so "would continue to be present" has been supplied implicitly. The propositional form thus attempts to indicate all the information implicit in the rather cryptic Greek, but it does not follow that every translation needs to give explicit expression to all of this information; the appropriate form for this sort of general prayer/benediction should be used.

3:17a–b I, Paul, am greeting *you and* I am writing *this* (3:17–18) myself Like 3:16b, there is a lot of implicit information in 3:17. In the Greek, what underlies 3:17a–b is Ὁ ἀσπασμὸς τῇ ἐμῇ χειρὶ Παύλου 'the greeting of Paul by my own hand'. Ὁ ἀσπασμός 'the greeting' is an abstract noun representing the event "to greet" so this is equivalent to "I, Paul, am greeting (you)." The phrase τῇ ἐμῇ χειρί 'by my own hand' indicates that Paul took the pen from his amanuensis at this point and wrote the greeting in his own handwriting—hence, the propositional form "and I am writing this myself." Paul was doing two things simultaneously—greeting the Thessalonian believers and actually penning the greeting. "By my own hand" is thus a metonymy for "I am writing this myself." It is also generally assumed that he then continued writing and wrote 3:18, as well.

Although the standard translation of "greeting" is used for ὁ ἀσπασμός, in normal English a greeting initiates a conversation, etc., not terminates it, as here. In Greek, "greetings" are an integral part of the *closing* of a letter, not its opening. It is clear from the narrative books of the New Testament that the corresponding verb, ἀσπάζομαι 'to greet', is used of *initial* greetings on arrival, etc. Hence, the preference of some for the (archaic) English "to salute" which does not have the component of "initial" in it. An expression in a translation which is only appropriate for initiating conversation, etc., should be avoided here; Paul is, in fact, signing off, and it corresponds more closely to the English "Yours sincerely" in function than the verb "to greet" would suggest.

3:17c–d *as I do* in all my letters *in order that* you may know *that I, Paul, have sent this letter.* Again, the Greek is cryptic: ὅ ἐστιν σημεῖον ἐν πάσῃ ἐπιστολῇ 'which is a sign in every letter'. Ὅ 'which' refers to his own personal writing of the greeting, and σημεῖον 'sign' in this context obviously means "a sign that the letter was written by me," i.e., that it is a genuine letter from Paul.

Paul is conscious of the claims of the source(s) of the false teaching referred to in 2:2 that they had the backing of a Pauline letter for their views.

Ἐν πάσῃ ἐπιστολῇ 'in every letter', however, is not so straightforward exegetically as it may appear. In the other Pauline letters, only 1 Corinthians (16:21) and Colossians (4:18) refer explicitly to Paul writing his own personal greeting. The generally preferred explanation is that Paul always wrote the closing of the letter himself, so that those who read it could see the obvious change in handwriting at the end, but that he only drew attention to that fact (and it should be remembered that most of the believers would only hear Paul's letters read out loud) when there was some reason to do so, as there obviously was here. This explanation is not without its difficulties—for example, there is no personal greeting from Paul at all in 2 Corinthians, but only from "all the saints"; where did he take over the writing himself, if he did?

What should the translator do? Since this is an exegetical question that only poses problems when all the Pauline letters are compared, and since it seems clear that he did mean in all the letters he wrote, it is recommended that the translator follow the display and simply say "in all my letters" or "in every letter that I write."

3:17e This is the way I write. The Greek is simply οὕτως γράφω 'thus I write', referring to his handwriting style, not to the content of what he says. It adds a (deictic) comment to 3:17b, and is probably added for emphasis, to draw attention to his (distinctive) handwriting style.

3:18 *We(exc)/I pray that* our(inc) Lord Jesus Christ *will continue to* act graciously to you all. The only real question here is how to handle the word χάρις 'grace'. The choice is between taking grace in its usual theological sense of "unmerited favor," or taking it in a more general sense of "bless/do good to," since it is being used in a standardized formula. All Paul's letters close with a prayer for grace for the readers; but there are variable additions, such as whether the Lord is referred to or not; whether it is "you" or "you all," etc., and there is also the rather expanded version at the end of 2 Corinthians. If a verb is used in the translation, it is essentially a prayer that the Lord Jesus would continue to act towards them in this way, and the tense/aspect chosen should reflect this.

BOUNDARIES AND COHERENCE

The case for the closing of the epistle beginning with the second half of 3:16 has already been argued in detail. The end of this epistle constituent coincides with the end of the total discourse.

Since the purpose of these verses is to bring the letter to an end, the things said are appropriate for that purpose—two prayers for the recipients and a personal greeting. The greeting is sandwiched between the two prayers, both of which are addressed (in effect) to the Lord Jesus Christ and ask for his blessing on all of the Thessalonian believers (ὁ κύριος 'the Lord' and πάντων ὑμῶν 'you all' in both prayers). The middle of the sandwich contains no less than three explicit references to Paul himself (contrast the use of "we" throughout the letter): ἐμῇ 'my', Παύλου 'of Paul', and γράφω 'I am writing'.

PROMINENCE AND THEME

The concept of a theme is difficult to apply to this epistle closing. The closing consists of three distinct constituents (see the display), but these constituents are related to each other only in that they are constituents of the closing. A central theme is not developed, but things are said which are appropriate to the end of a letter. This juxtaposing of independent, but appropriate constituents, is characteristic of the closing of an epistle; (see also the discussion of the boundaries and coherence of 3:16a).

There is no evidence on the basis of which any one of the three constituents could be analyzed as more prominent than the other two, so they are regarded as conjoined and of equal semantic importance. While no theme is developed, it is clear from the display that Paul and his colleagues pray for the Thessalonian believers (3:16b and 18), and Paul personally greets the Thessalonians and authenticates the letter. The two prayers can readily be combined into the more generic prayer: "We(exc) pray that our(inc) Lord Jesus will bless you all." This prayer can then be added to the two main propositions and the purpose in the propositional cluster, 3:17a-e, to give a summary of the main information conveyed in the epistle closing.

BIBLIOGRAPHY

Commentaries and SSAs

Alford, Henry. 1880. *The Greek Testament*, Vol. III. Rivingtons/Deighton: Bell and Co.

Beekman, John; and Smith, Robert E. 1981. *A Literary-Semantic Analysis of Second Timothy*. Dallas, TX: Summer Institute of Linguistics.

Best, Ernest. 1979. *A Commentary on the First and Second Epistles to the Thessalonians*. London: Adam and Charles Black.

Blight, Richard. 1977. "A Literary-Semantic Analysis of Paul's First Discourse to Timothy." Prepublication draft.

Eadie, John. 1979. *Commentary on the Greek Text of the Epistles of Paul to the Thessalonians*. Edited by William Young. Reprint of 1877 edition. Grand Rapids, Mich.: Baker Book House.

Ellicott, C. J. 1858. *A Critical and Grammatical Commentary on St. Paul's Epistles to the Thessalonians*. London: John W. Parker and Son.

Ellingworth, Paul, and Eugene A. Nida. 1976. *A Translator's Handbook on Paul's Letters to the Thessalonians*. United Bible Society.

Giblin, Charles H. 1967. *The Threat to Faith. An exegetical and theological re-examination of 2 Thessalonians 2*. Rome: Pontifical Biblical Institute.

Hendriksen, William. 1955. *New Testament Commentary: Exposition of 1 and 2 Thessalonians*. Grand Rapids: Baker Book House.

Kopesec, Michael F. 1980. *A Literary-Semantic Analysis of Titus* (preliminary edition). Dallas: Summer Institute of Linguistics.

Morris, Leon. 1959. *The First and Second Epistles to the Thessalonians*. London/Edinburgh: Marshall, Morgan and Scott, Ltd.

Lünemann, Gottlieb. 1880. *Critical and Exegetical Commentary on the New Testament: The Epistles to the Thessalonians*. Edinburgh: T. and T. Clark.

Versions and Texts

Good News for Modern Man. The New Testament in Today's English Version. 1966. New York: The Bible Society.

Goodspeed, Edgar J. 1948. *The New Testament: An American Translation*. Chicago: University of Chicago Press.

The Holy Bible. Authorized (or King James) Version. 1611.

The Holy Bible. Revised Standard Version. 1952.

Knox, Ronald A. 1953. *The New Testament*. New York: Sheed and Ward.

Metzger, Bruce M. 1971. *A Textual Commentary on the Greek New Testament*. London/New York: United Bible Societies.

Moffat, James. 1935. *A New Translation of the Bible*. Revised edition. New York: Harper and Brothers.

The New English Bible Testament. 1961. Oxford/Cambridge.

Phillips, J. B. 1958. *The New Testament in Modern English*. New York: Macmillan Company.

Pierpont, W. G. 1977. *The Majority Text of the Greek New Testament*. Mimeographed edition.

Taylor, Kenneth N. *Living Letters*. Wheaton, IL: Tyndale House.

The Twentieth Century New Testament. 1904. Revised edition. New York: Fleming H. Revell.

United Bible Society. 1975. *The Greek New Testament*. Third edition.

Verkuyl, Gerrit. 1945. *Berkeley Version of the New Testament*. Berkeley, Calif.: James J. Gillick and Co.

Weymouth, Richard Francis. 1943. *The New Testament in Modern Speech*. 5th ed. revised by J. A. Robertson, 1929. Boston: Pilgrim Press.

Reference Works

Abbott-Smith, G. 1956. *Manual Greek Lexicon of the New Testament*. Edinburgh: T. and T. Clark.

Alsop, John R. 1964. *Index to the Arndt and Gingrich Greek Lexicon*. Santa Ana, Calif.: Wycliffe Bible Translators.

Arndt, William F., and Wilbur F. Gingrich. 1952. *A Greek-English Lexicon of the New Testament and Other Early Christian Literature*. Chicago: University of Chicago Press.

Beekman, John, and John Callow. 1974. *Translating the Word of God*. Grand Rapids: Zondervan.

Beekman, John, John Callow, and Michael F. Kopesec. 1981. *The Semantic Structure of Written Communication*. 5th rev. Dallas: SIL.

Blass, F., and A. Debrunner. 1961. *A Greek Grammar of the New Testament*. A translation and revision of the ninth-tenth German edition by Robert W. Funk. Chicago: University of Chicago Press.

Burton, Ernest de Witt. 1978. *Syntax of the Moods and Tenses in New Testament Greek*. Reprint of the 1900 edition. Grand Rapids: Kregel.

Douglas, J. D., editor. 1977. *The New Bible Dictionary*. Inter Varsity Press.

Friberg, Timothy. 1982. "New Testament Greek Word Order in Light of Discourse Considerations." Ph.D. thesis submitted to the University of Minnesota.

Hanna, Robert. 1980. *A Grammatical Aid to the Greek New Testament*, Vol. II (Romans to Revelation).

Moule, C. F. D. 1960. *An Idiom-Book of New Testament Greek*. Cambridge: Cambridge University Press.

Robertson, A. T. 1931. *Word Pictures in the New Testament*. Nashville: Broadman Press.

———. *A Grammar of the Greek New Testament in the Light of Historical Research*. Nashville: Broadman Press.

Turner, Nigel. 1963. *Syntax. A Grammar of New Testament Greek*. Edinburgh: T. and T. Clark.

Articles

Aus, Roger D. 1973. "The liturgical background of the necessity and propriety of giving thanks according to 2 Thess. 1:3." *Journal of Biblical Literature*, 92:3.

Barnouin, M. 1977. "Les problemes de traduction concernant 2 Thessalonians 2:6-7." *New Testament Studies*, July 1977, 23:4, pp. 482-98.

Bell Robert D. 1975. "Practical exhortations concerning disciplinary separation." *Biblical Viewpoint*, Nov. 1975, 9:2, pp. 92-96. Greenville, SC: Bob Jones University.

Custer, Stewart. 1975. "Characteristics of the tribulation." *Biblical Viewpoint*, Nov. 1975, 9:2, pp. 82-84. Greenville, SC: Bob Jones University.

Minn, H. R. 1975. "Effective techniques in Pauline diction." *Prudentia*, Nov. 1975, 7:2, pp. 89-93.

www.ingramcontent.com/pod-product-compliance
Lightning Source LLC
Chambersburg PA
CBHW080739230426
43665CB00020B/2795